CAROL VORDERMAN
Maths Made Easy

10
Minutes
A Day
Decimals

Author and Consultant
Sean McArdle

Ages
7–11

DK

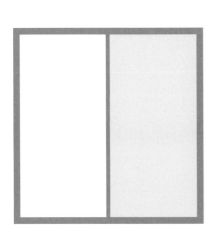
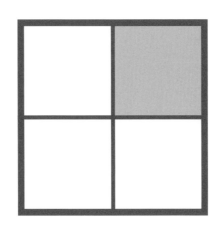
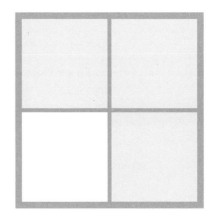

T0354090

10-minute challenge

Try to complete the exercises for each topic in 10 minutes or less. Note the time it takes you in the "Time taken" column below.

DK London
Editors Elizabeth Blakemore, Jolyon Goddard
Senior Editor Deborah Lock
Managing Editor Christine Stroyan
Managing Art Editor Anna Hall
Maths Consultant Sean McArdle
Senior Production Editor Andy Hilliard
Senior Production Controller Jude Crozier
Jacket Design Development Manager Sophia MTT
Publisher Andrew Macintyre
Associate Publishing Director Liz Wheeler
Art Director Karen Self
Publishing Director Jonathan Metcalf

DK Delhi
Senior Editor Rupa Rao
Art Editor Jyotsna Julka
Managing Editors Soma B. Chowdhury,
Kingshuk Ghoshal
Managing Art Editors Ahlawat Gunjan, Govind Mittal
DTP Designers Anita Yadav, Rakesh Kumar,
Harish Aggarwal
Senior Jacket Designer Suhita Dharamjit
Jackets Editorial Coordinator Priyanka Sharma

This edition published in 2020
First published in Great Britain in 2015 by
Dorling Kindersley Limited
20 Vauxhall Bridge Road,
London SW1V 2SA

The authorised representative in the EEA is
Dorling Kindersley Verlag GmbH. Arnulfstr. 124,
80636 Munich, Germany

A CIP catalogue record for this book
is available from the British Library.
ISBN: 978-0-2411-8233-8

Printed and bound in China

All images © Dorling Kindersley

www.dk.com

This book was made with Forest
Stewardship Council™ certified
paper - one small step in DK's
commitment to a sustainable future.
**For more information go to
www.dk.com/our-green-pledge**

Contents

Time taken

4

Equivalents 1

Just like fractions, decimal numbers can be used to show the proportion of a whole.

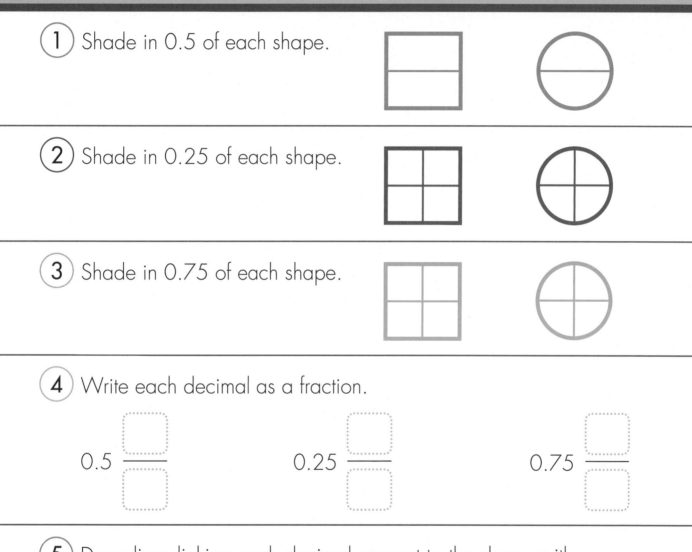

① Shade in 0.5 of each shape.

② Shade in 0.25 of each shape.

③ Shade in 0.75 of each shape.

④ Write each decimal as a fraction.

0.5 $\frac{}{}$

0.25 $\frac{}{}$

0.75 $\frac{}{}$

⑤ Draw lines linking each decimal amount to the shape with the equivalent area shaded.

0.5

0.25

0.75

Time filler:
Look at questions 6 and 7 again. But this time, what decimal amount has been left unshaded? Do you have a chessboard? What decimal amount of the squares is black and what amount is white?

6 What decimal amount of each shape has been shaded?

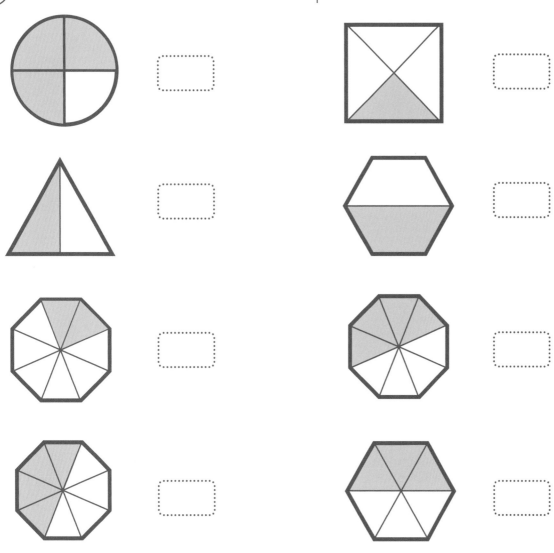

7 Write the corresponding decimal for each shaded portion.

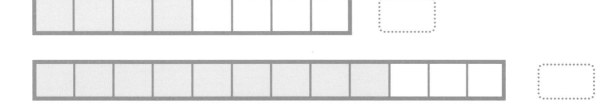

Equivalents 2

Fractions can also be written as decimals,
and decimals can be written as fractions.

(1) Write each fraction as a decimal.

$\frac{1}{10}$ ☐ $\frac{1}{100}$ ☐ $\frac{3}{10}$ ☐ $\frac{7}{100}$ ☐

$\frac{6}{10}$ ☐ $\frac{9}{10}$ ☐ $\frac{3}{100}$ ☐ $\frac{9}{100}$ ☐

$\frac{6}{100}$ ☐ $\frac{5}{10}$ ☐ $\frac{8}{100}$ ☐ $\frac{2}{100}$ ☐

$\frac{2}{10}$ ☐ $\frac{4}{10}$ ☐ $\frac{7}{10}$ ☐ $\frac{4}{100}$ ☐

$\frac{12}{10}$ ☐ $\frac{68}{100}$ ☐ $\frac{23}{100}$ ☐ $\frac{10}{100}$ ☐

$\frac{45}{10}$ ☐ $\frac{32}{100}$ ☐ $\frac{51}{10}$ ☐ $\frac{97}{100}$ ☐

$\frac{61}{100}$ ☐ $\frac{18}{10}$ ☐ $\frac{33}{10}$ ☐ $\frac{75}{100}$ ☐

$\frac{28}{10}$ ☐ $\frac{87}{10}$ ☐ $\frac{66}{100}$ ☐ $\frac{22}{100}$ ☐

$\frac{52}{100}$ ☐ $\frac{19}{10}$ ☐ $\frac{73}{100}$ ☐ $\frac{92}{10}$ ☐

Time filler:
Think of ten numbers between 1 and 99.
Write each of these numbers as the numerator
(top number) in a fraction, with 10 as the
denominator (lower number) and then 100 as
the denominator. Now write these 20 fractions
as their equivalent decimals.

② Write each decimal as a fraction.

0.08 ⬜/⬜   0.15 ⬜/⬜   0.06 ⬜/⬜   0.27 ⬜/⬜   0.9 ⬜/⬜

0.34 ⬜/⬜   0.57 ⬜/⬜   0.05 ⬜/⬜   0.97 ⬜/⬜   0.02 ⬜/⬜

0.62 ⬜/⬜   0.48 ⬜/⬜   0.23 ⬜/⬜   0.71 ⬜/⬜   0.6 ⬜/⬜

0.01 ⬜/⬜   0.1 ⬜/⬜   0.5 ⬜/⬜   0.68 ⬜/⬜   0.7 ⬜/⬜

0.25 ⬜/⬜   0.75 ⬜/⬜   0.3 ⬜/⬜   0.03 ⬜/⬜   0.8 ⬜/⬜

Dividing by 10 and 100

Decimal comes from the Latin word *decimus*, meaning "tenth". Can you see why?

---

1 Write whether 1 is in the ten, unit, tenth or hundredth place in these numbers.

1.0	0.1	0.01	2.1	32.01
....	....	....	....	....

4.12	21.8	7.1	1.2	10.6
....	....	....	....	....

---

2 Suki has a total of £13.68 in her piggy bank. Which part of that number is the unit place and which is the tenth place?

Unit [ ]

Tenth [ ]

---

3 Divide each number by 10 and write the answer in the decimal form.

50 [ ]   4 [ ]   81 [ ]   70 [ ]   25 [ ]

7 [ ]   35 [ ]   60 [ ]   90 [ ]   5 [ ]

15 [ ]   11 [ ]   18 [ ]   20 [ ]   32 [ ]

Time filler:
Write down the ages of everyone in your family. Include grandparents if your family is small. Divide all of their ages by 10. Then repeat the exercise, this time dividing all their ages by 100. Use decimals in your answers.

(4) Divide each number by 100 and write the answer in the decimal form.

78 [ ]   12 [ ]   43 [ ]   9 [ ]   99 [ ]

40 [ ]   5 [ ]   66 [ ]   1 [ ]   50 [ ]

32 [ ]   10 [ ]   70 [ ]   55 [ ]   92 [ ]

(5) Write whether 5 is in the ten, unit, tenth or hundredth place in these numbers.

56.3   7.05   0.5   5.62   0.05

....

15.2   12.5   51.9   20.5   5.78

....

(6) Write whether 8 is in the unit, tenth or hundredth place in these numbers.

7.68   8.6   9.83   12.08   8.43

....

4.81   10.8   8.24   6.38   18.5

....

Rounding decimals

Decimal numbers ending in .5 are always
rounded upwards, not downwards.

1 Round each decimal to the nearest whole number.

6.3	[ ]	7.6 [ ]	9.8 [ ]

6.3 [   ]   7.6 [   ]   9.8 [   ]

4.2 [   ]   0.5 [   ]   24.5 [   ]

24.9 [   ]   15.5 [   ]   15.7 [   ]

42.5 [   ]   12.1 [   ]   49.8 [   ]

18.2 [   ]   56.4 [   ]   79.5 [   ]

17.3 [   ]   89.5 [   ]   57.7 [   ]

93.9 [   ]   69.9 [   ]   87.9 [   ]

88.4 [   ]   88.5 [   ]   88.6 [   ]

68.5 [   ]   85.6 [   ]   65.8 [   ]

32.7 [   ]   73.3 [   ]   88.8 [   ]

90.5 [   ]   42.6 [   ]   59.1 [   ]

40.5 [   ]   52.5 [   ]   73.4 [   ]

Time filler:
Find two of your favourite books. Measure the length, width and depth (thickness) of each book as accurately as possible with a ruler. Now round these numbers to the nearest centimetre.

(2) Round each decimal to the nearest whole unit.

4.5 cm	3.8 m	7.1 km
56.4 g	2.3 kg	12.5 g
66.6 m	86.5 mm	42.8 kg
47.6 cm	17.3 cm	19.1 km
15.5 cm	81.7 mm	23.7 kg
14.2 g	56.5 m	68.8 km
49.2 m	35.7 cm	26.6 mm
76.4 m	76.5 cm	76.6 mm
67.5 g	57.2 kg	57.7 km

(3) Caleb's favourite book is 21.2 cm wide, 30.5 cm long and 1.9 cm thick. Round these measurements to the nearest centimetre.

Comparing decimals 1

Is there a point to decimal numbers?
Yes, it's called the decimal point!

① Circle the larger number in each pair.

3.6 6.3	4.8 8.4	3.5 3.8	9.0 8.9
5.3 4.9	8.0 6.9	12.3 13.3	23.3 33.2
21.2 22.1	35.8 58.3	18.6 16.8	31.5 35.1
2.9 9.2	1.5 2.5	19.8 18.9	34.1 33.9
80.1 80.9	26.3 23.6	14.7 17.4	55.4 54.5

② Circle the smallest number in each group.

23.2 22.3 23.3	48.7 47.8 48.8	54.6 56.4 54.5

③ Circle the largest number in each group.

28.3 23.8 28.2	95.5 59.5 55.9	63.4 64.3 63.2

Time filler:
Find six objects in the kitchen, such as a mug, jam jar, fork, spoon, potato, carrot, etc. Pair up those of a similar size. Measure the longest side of each item with a ruler and write down the lengths, with the pairs together. Now circle the shorter length in each pair.

4 Circle the smaller amount in each pair.

| 24.6 mm 26.4 mm | £2.58   £2.85 | 17.9 m   19.7 m |

| 5.48 mm 5.84 mm | 17.25 cm 12.75 cm | 24.82 g 28.42 g |

| 0.67 g   0.76 g | 1.89 cm   1.98 cm | 3.83 g   3.38 g |

| 29.4 cm 49.2 cm | 34.3 mm 33.4 mm | 97.8 g   98.7 g |

| 2.41 g   4.21 g | 0.58 cm 1.29 cm | 9.09 g   9.13 g |

5 Circle the larger amount in each pair.

| 8.09 g   8.9 g | 8.8 m   0.65 m | 0.56 cm 1.01 cm |

6 Circle the smallest amount in each group.

| 18.06 m   18.04 m   18.1 m | 36.67 kg 37.67 kg 36.66 kg |

Measurements and money

14

We use decimal numbers all the time.
Weights, lengths and amounts of
money are often written as decimals.

(1) Alex runs 1.82 km, Mike runs
1.28 km and Harris runs 1.56 km.
Who runs farther than Harris?

....

(2) Answer these questions.

How much longer is 1.45 m than 1.35 m?

Which weighs more, 2.56 kg or 2.65 kg?

Which of these measurements is the same as 108 cm?

10.8 m   1.8 m   1.08 m

(3) Clara has 0.4 kg of fruit; Katie has double
that amount. How much fruit does Katie have?

David has half Clara's amount.
How much fruit does David have?

(4) Roisin believes 186 cm is the same as
1.86 m. Is she correct?

....

Olly says 190 cm is 10 cm less than
2 m. Is he correct?

....

Time filler:
Empty your piggy bank or money box. Put all the different coins – 1 penny, 2 pence, 5 pence, 10 pence, etc. – into separate piles and count each pile. Write them down in the decimal format, for example: £0.67, and add them all together. Did you have more or less money than you expected?

(5) Write each amount in pence.

£3.50

£2.28

£0.67

£10.40

£1.45

£1.54

£4.51

£5.14

(6) Write each amount as pounds.

467 p

273 p

95 p

608 p

384 p

529 p

77 p

999 p

(7) Write each amount in pounds and pence.

Three hundred and fifty-five pounds and twenty-five pence

Two hundred and thirty pounds and forty-five pence

(8) Garry's pencil is 12.65 cm long, Larry's pencil is 12.56 cm long and Harry's pencil is 12.60 cm long. Who has the shortest pencil?

Equivalents 3

They will look different, but many decimals can also be written as fractions.

Place each of these fractions in the correct place on the number lines.

① $\frac{4}{5}$ $\frac{3}{5}$ $\frac{1}{5}$

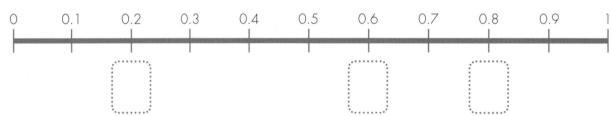

② $\frac{3}{10}$ $\frac{5}{10}$ $\frac{9}{10}$

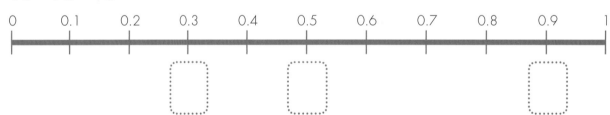

③ $\frac{7}{10}$ $\frac{1}{10}$ $\frac{8}{10}$

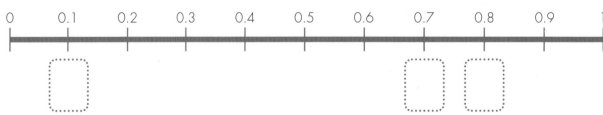

④ $\frac{4}{10}$ $\frac{6}{10}$ $\frac{2}{10}$

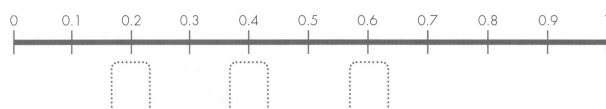

Time filler:
Draw a 10-cm line on a piece of paper and make a mark at the 0.5 (i.e. halfway) position along its length. Draw a 20-cm line and make marks at the 0.25, 0.5 and 0.75 positions. Finally, draw a 30-cm line and make marks at the 0.1, 0.4, 0.6 and 0.9 positions.

(5) $\frac{70}{100}$ $\frac{90}{100}$ $\frac{20}{100}$

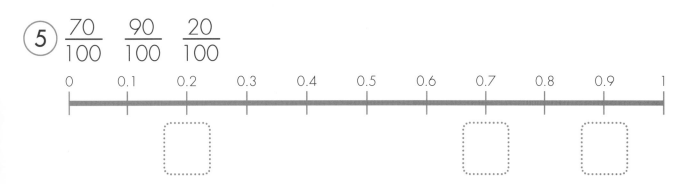

(6) $\frac{10}{100}$ $\frac{80}{100}$ $\frac{50}{100}$

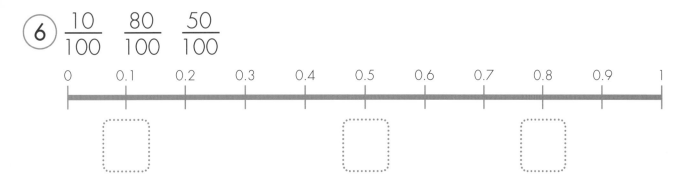

(7) $\frac{35}{100}$ $\frac{65}{100}$ $\frac{95}{100}$

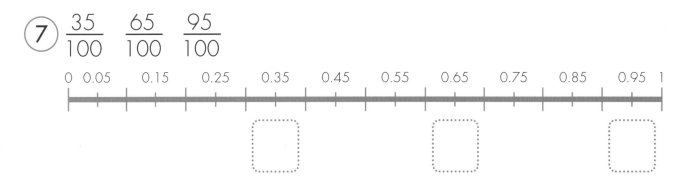

(8) $\frac{15}{100}$ $\frac{85}{100}$ $\frac{55}{100}$

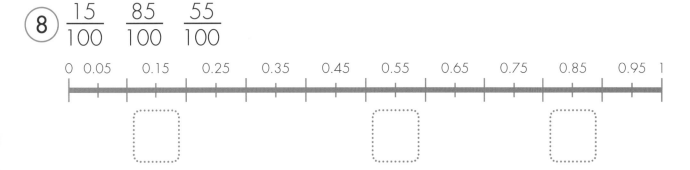

Equivalents 4

What do you prefer – fractions
or decimals? Let's practise
them both!

① Write each fraction in its decimal form.

$\frac{345}{1000}$ ☐ $\frac{250}{1000}$ ☐ $\frac{476}{1000}$ ☐ $\frac{132}{1000}$ ☐

$\frac{781}{1000}$ ☐ $\frac{908}{1000}$ ☐ $\frac{285}{1000}$ ☐ $\frac{719}{1000}$ ☐

$\frac{46}{1000}$ ☐ $\frac{83}{1000}$ ☐ $\frac{98}{1000}$ ☐ $\frac{66}{1000}$ ☐

$\frac{51}{1000}$ ☐ $\frac{90}{1000}$ ☐ $\frac{81}{1000}$ ☐ $\frac{75}{1000}$ ☐

$\frac{10}{1000}$ ☐ $\frac{5}{1000}$ ☐ $\frac{20}{1000}$ ☐ $\frac{1}{1000}$ ☐

$\frac{29}{1000}$ ☐ $\frac{459}{1000}$ ☐ $\frac{205}{1000}$ ☐ $\frac{853}{1000}$ ☐

$\frac{231}{1000}$ ☐ $\frac{85}{1000}$ ☐ $\frac{397}{1000}$ ☐ $\frac{59}{1000}$ ☐

$\frac{109}{1000}$ ☐ $\frac{27}{1000}$ ☐ $\frac{720}{1000}$ ☐ $\frac{18}{1000}$ ☐

Time filler:
Here is some extra practice with units: how many metres (m) are there in one kilometre (km)? How many centimetres (cm) are there in 1 km? And how many millimetres (mm) are there in 1 km?

2) Write each decimal as a fraction.

0.645 ⬚/⬚ 0.629 ⬚/⬚ 0.173 ⬚/⬚ 0.615 ⬚/⬚

0.03 ⬚/⬚ 0.004 ⬚/⬚ 0.6 ⬚/⬚ 0.07 ⬚/⬚

0.19 ⬚/⬚ 0.001 ⬚/⬚ 0.429 ⬚/⬚ 0.8 ⬚/⬚

3) How much is 0.01 of 1 km? Answer in metres. ⬚

How much is 0.001 of 1 kg? Answer in grams. ⬚

4) How much is 0.01 of 1 l? Answer in millilitres.

⬚

How much is 0.001 of 10 km? Answer in metres.

⬚

Beat the clock 1

Test your decimals knowledge.
Get started now!

Write each fraction in its decimal form.

(1) $\frac{1}{4}$ [ ] (2) $\frac{3}{4}$ [ ] (3) $\frac{1}{2}$ [ ]

(4) $\frac{2}{5}$ [ ] (5) $\frac{4}{5}$ [ ] (6) $\frac{1}{5}$ [ ]

(7) $\frac{3}{5}$ [ ] (8) $\frac{9}{10}$ [ ] (9) $\frac{1}{10}$ [ ]

(10) $\frac{7}{10}$ [ ] (11) $\frac{4}{10}$ [ ] (12) $\frac{5}{10}$ [ ]

(13) $\frac{6}{10}$ [ ] (14) $\frac{8}{10}$ [ ] (15) $\frac{3}{10}$ [ ]

Divide each number by 10.

(16) 7 [ ] (17) 18 [ ] (18) 12 [ ]

(19) 21 [ ] (20) 2 [ ] (21) 5 [ ]

(22) 11 [ ] (23) 30 [ ] (24) 50 [ ]

(25) 6 [ ] (26) 400 [ ] (27) 150 [ ]

(28) 360 [ ] (29) 700 [ ] (30) 490 [ ]

Time filler:
Can you work out $\frac{1}{8}$ as a decimal?
Now see if you can work out $\frac{3}{8}$, $\frac{5}{8}$
and $\frac{7}{8}$ as decimals, too.

Round each number to two decimal places.

(31) 5.671 ⬚　　(32) 4.968 ⬚　　(33) 1.635 ⬚

(34) 8.524 ⬚　　(35) 12.965 ⬚　　(36) 1.345 ⬚

(37) 8.046 ⬚　　(38) 9.432 ⬚　　(39) 0.657 ⬚

Round each number to the nearest whole number.

(40) 6.8 ⬚　　(41) 7.9 ⬚　　(42) 3.1 ⬚

(43) 7.5 ⬚　　(44) 8.3 ⬚　　(45) 9.7 ⬚

(46) 21.5 ⬚　　(47) 36.5 ⬚　　(48) 3.6 ⬚

Write each decimal as a fraction.

(49) 0.75 ⬚　　(50) 0.96 ⬚　　(51) 0.02 ⬚

(52) 0.25 ⬚　　(53) 0.675 ⬚　　(54) 0.008 ⬚

(55) 0.30 ⬚　　(56) 0.003 ⬚　　(57) 0.5 ⬚

Addition 1

Don't forget to include the number
(tenths) after the decimal point
when doing these sums.

(1) Find the totals.

$3 + 1.5 =$ [_____]

$5 + 2.5 =$ [_____]

$8.3 + 4 =$ [_____]

$6.4 + 5 =$ [_____]

$7 + 0.2 =$ [_____]

$1 + 1.4 =$ [_____]

$6.9 + 3 =$ [_____]

$5 + 2.2 =$ [_____]

$7.4 + 3 =$ [_____]

$12.3 + 8 =$ [_____]

$2.4 + 6 =$ [_____]

$4.4 + 6 =$ [_____]

$12 + 8.6 =$ [_____]

$17.4 + 3 =$ [_____]

$18.7 + 6 =$ [_____]

$7.3 + 7 =$ [_____]

$14 + 0.7 =$ [_____]

$24 + 0.3 =$ [_____]

(2) On holiday, Richard spent 3 days in France,
0.5 days in Luxembourg, 2.5 days in Belgium
and 3.5 days in the Netherlands. How long
was Richard's holiday?

[_____] days

Time filler:
When you add all the different British notes and coins together, what is the total? (Hint: they are £50, £20, £10, £5, £2, £1, 50p, 20p, 10p, 5p, 2p and 1p.)

(3) Find the totals.

3 + 4.6 + 2 =

6 + 8 + 3.5 =

6.3 + 4 + 4 =

8 + 3.9 + 3 =

4.6 + 4 + 6 =

9.1 + 9 + 2 =

3.4 + 5 + 6 =

7 + 6.3 + 4 =

6 + 4.3 + 12 =

4.8 + 6 + 9 =

7 + 2.2 + 8 =

4 + 7 + 6.9 =

1.2 + 3 + 5 =

6 + 4 + 0.1 =

4.5 + 6 + 3 =

7.9 + 1 + 3 =

0.9 + 1 + 7 =

0.6 + 4 + 5 =

8 + 9 + 5.4 =

6.6 + 6 + 6 =

5.1 + 9 + 3 =

17 + 3 + 0.2 =

12 + 7 + 5.9 =

24 + 8 + 0.8 =

Addition 2

Don't be scared of the decimal point!
It's there to help us write numbers as
accurately as possible.

(1) Write the answers.

2.5 m + 4 m = [ ]

17 m + 2.8 m = [ ]

4.3 g + 9.4 g = [ ]

6.2 g + 4.1 g = [ ]

7.1 m + 3.4 m = [ ]

3 cm + 4.2 cm = [ ]

12 cm + 4.8 cm = [ ]

6.3 kg + 9.6 kg = [ ]

8 mm + 2.4 mm = [ ]

5.9 g + 7 g = [ ]

7 g + 4.3 g = [ ]

9.5 g + 5 g = [ ]

1.8 kg + 3 kg = [ ]

6.5 g + 4.4 g = [ ]

8 km + 3.4 km = [ ]

12.5 g + 3.4 g = [ ]

8.5 ml + 6.3 ml = [ ]

3.7 ml + 2.2 ml = [ ]

(2) Kim and Harry plant some flowers in their garden.
$2.75 \, m^2$ of the area is planted with
roses and $1.5 \, m^2$ of it with daisies.
What is the total area
planted with flowers?

[ ]

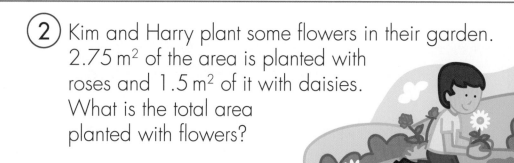

Time filler:
Write some more challenges for yourself and your parents. For example, what is the answer to £3.15 + £4.22 + £8.19 or 6.3 m + 8.2 m + 3.3 m? Try to make up ten new sums with decimal amounts.

(3) Martin needs £25.75 for a new bicycle wheel. He does a few odd jobs for family and neighbours and earns £8.15, £5.20, £3.23 and £9.50. How much money does Martin have now?

(4) Find the total amounts.

£2.56 + £2.56 = [ ]   £1.62 + £0.20 = [ ]

£4.20 + £0.50 = [ ]   £6.50 + £1.30 = [ ]

£6.75 + £0.20 = [ ]   £8.66 + £1.10 = [ ]

£3.33 + £2.60 = [ ]   £5.50 + £3.25 = [ ]

£6.20 + £3.75 = [ ]   £8.10 + £2.25 = [ ]

£5.35 + £4.25 = [ ]   £7.50 + £5.15 = [ ]

£3.00 + £2.50 + £1.30 = [ ]   £6.10 + £2.30 + £1.25 = [ ]

£0.25 + £0.25 + £0.25 = [ ]   £1.23 + £4.00 + £3.20 = [ ]

£1.08 + £2.03 + £6.00 = [ ]   £1.90 + £3.00 + £2.10 = [ ]

Comparing decimals 2

When comparing decimal numbers, read them very carefully. For example: 2.333 is just one-thousandth smaller than 2.334.

1 Circle the larger number in each pair.

| 3.6   1.9 | 5.86   5.68 | 7.674 7.688 | 1.03   1.003 |

2 Circle the smaller number in each pair.

| 2.05   2.48 | 3.867 3.847 | 5.231   4.999 | 5.051 5.105 |

3 Rewrite each row in order, starting with the smallest number.

| 3.756 | 3.75 | 3.675 | 3.57 |

| 4.086 | 4.085 | 4.058 | 4.068 |

| 12.3 | 11.9 | 13.867 | 11.444 |

| 8.23 | 3.82 | 2.83 | 3.28 |

Time filler:
Measure your height and that of a few of your friends or family members. Measure to the nearest millimetre if possible. Then write the heights in order, with the tallest first.

4 Circle the larger amount in each pair.

| 6.72 cm   6.27 cm | 4.88 g   4.91 g | 6.03 m   3.6 m |

5 Circle the smaller amount in each pair.

| 8.326 kg   8.623 kg | 4.845 km   3.999 km | 5.123 m   5.104 m |

6 Rewrite each row in order, starting with the largest amount.

| 4.867 km | 4.881 km | 6.496 km | 4.904 km |

| 18.826 kg | 12.978 kg | 31.423 kg | 31.4 kg |

| £7.49 | £7.40 | £8.00 | £7.94 |

| £15.67 | £18.23 | £15.76 | £17.78 |

Addition 3

How quickly can you solve these sums?
Concentrate… and go!

(1) Add the numbers.

3.6 + 2.8 = [ ]   4.4 + 9.3 = [ ]   7.6 + 2.9 = [ ]

6.25 + 4.4 = [ ]   4.4 + 18.3 = [ ]   7.2 + 11.2 = [ ]

3.71 + 8.81 = [ ]   4.55 + 1.25 = [ ]   3.05 + 2.05 = [ ]

8.92 + 4.19 = [ ]   3.85 + 1.05 = [ ]   12.3 + 3.8 = [ ]

6.12 + 2.08 = [ ]   13.7 + 2.4 = [ ]   29.5 + 6.2 = [ ]

(2) Find the totals.

3.0 + 6.1 + 7.3 = [ ]   7.3 + 2.4 + 1.6 = [ ]

5.4 + 3.2 + 1.0 = [ ]   2.8 + 6.5 + 3.2 = [ ]

6.7 + 3.9 + 4.9 = [ ]   8.2 + 5.0 + 3.8 = [ ]

4.9 + 8.8 + 1.4 = [ ]   6.5 + 4.5 + 3.5 = [ ]

12.2 + 4.4 + 10.0 = [ ]   13.2 + 5.5 + 12.6 = [ ]

Time filler:
Can you do these sums in your head?
5.5 + 4.5
12.25 + 7.75
15.51 + 14.49
How did you do?

(3) Work out the answers.

4.6 + 3.4	5.6 + 6.8	7.1 + 3.4	9.3 + 1.4	6.1 + 4.8
....	....	....	....	....
12.8 + 6.7	11.6 + 4.7	15.3 + 2.9	24.7 + 3.3	64.8 + 7.4
....	....	....	....	....
4.63 + 1.27	5.89 + 2.33	1.07 + 2.46	4.36 + 1.44	8.26 + 1.74
....	....	....	....	....
60.34 + 31.47	31.23 + 14.56	56.12 + 21.08	23.99 + 12.01	33.93 + 83.72
....	....	....	....	....

(4) Each morning, Zara and Kyle walk 0.35 km to the bus stop, travel 3.85 km on the bus and then walk 0.25 km to reach their school. How far is their journey?

Addition 4

Always double check your
answers when working out sums
as it helps overcome mistakes.

① Find the totals.

$3.48 + 5.52 =$ ⬚ $1.09 + 0.91 =$ ⬚

$3.0 + 6.464 =$ ⬚ $4.89 + 2.11 =$ ⬚

$6.042 + 1.1 =$ ⬚ $5.109 + 7.9 =$ ⬚

$5.64 + 2.364 =$ ⬚ $2.34 + 4.001 =$ ⬚

$7.25 + 3.593 =$ ⬚ $7.62 + 3.041 =$ ⬚

② Work out these addition sums.

```
   2.65        1.783        6.20         9.132        2.391
+  1.46      + 2.620     +  3.88      +  1.410     +  0.129
───────      ───────     ───────      ───────      ───────
...........   ...........   ...........   ...........   ...........

  52.60       81.230       56.902       7.008        4.150
+  8.23      +  3.284     + 6.700      + 0.830      + 1.213
───────      ───────     ───────      ───────      ───────
...........   ...........   ...........   ...........   ...........

  23.600       0.600       12.850       4.94         6.403
+  0.123     + 3.567      + 9.006      + 0.70       + 4.892
───────      ───────     ───────      ───────      ───────
...........   ...........   ...........   ...........   ...........
```

Time filler:
Measure the lengths of the fingers and thumb on one of your hands to the nearest millimetre. Add the lengths together and write your answer in centimetres.

(3) Answer these questions.

How much is £3.56 plus £2.99?

What is 1.56 m added to 1.86 m?

How much is 1.675 km increased by 0.255 km?

What amount is £2.67 more than £12.50?

(4) A kitchen worktop is made up of two pieces. One piece is 1.645 m long and the other 0.546 m. What will be the length of the whole worktop when the two pieces are joined together?

(5) What is the total when £2.85 is added to each of these?

£2.69   £4.50

(6) Add this group of numbers and write the total.

2.455   7.234   8.167

Addition 5

Try these sums. They are slightly harder. Are you ready for the challenge?

① A car makes three journeys. The first journey is 8.627 km, the second is 9.348 km and the third is 12.450 km. How far does the car travel in total?

> [....]

② Write the answers.

2.423	1.867	0.655	7.291
+ 1.534	+ 2.427	+ 2.809	+ 0.810

0.836	2.056	7.340	4.980
+ 6.190	+ 1.006	+ 8.455	+ 2.713

4.006	3.501	2.956	12.535
+ 1.040	+ 0.660	+ 0.300	+ 6.375

10.044	12.800	6.834	9.471
2.860	0.640	1.423	1.250
+ 8.009	+ 4.235	+ 0.223	+ 3.089

Time filler:
Here's an extra question. At lunch, Nate spent £3.25 on a sandwich, £1.30 on a drink, 65p on a snack and 42p on an apple. How much did he spend in total?

3) Find the totals.

4.6 + 3.4 =

6.6 + 3.9 =

7.3 + 4.1 =

7.9 + 2.2 =

5.6 + 12.8 =

1.2 + 3.9 =

3.8 + 4.21 =

3.45 + 0.45 =

12.5 + 6.5 =

4.65 + 0.25 =

8.22 + 7.33 =

2.065 + 0.023 =

1.2 + 3.4 + 2.6 =

5.6 + 2.3 + 5.3 =

6.3 + 0.5 + 4.3 =

7.5 + 4.5 + 3.5 =

7.1 + 8.2 + 9.3 =

7.0 + 6.72 + 2.45 =

4) Cressida ran 2.50 km on Monday, 7.01 km on Wednesday and 3.09 km on Saturday. What is the total distance she ran during that week?

Decimals, fractions and percentages

Like fractions, percentages are also equivalent to decimals. For example: 0.5 is equivalent to both $\frac{1}{2}$ and 50%.

(1) What is 25% of each number?

8.4 [   ]   12.0 [   ]   6.4 [   ]   20.4 [   ]

6.0 [   ]   9.2 [   ]   16.8 [   ]   440.0 [   ]

(2) What is 50% of each number?

3.0 [   ]   7.0 [   ]   1.2 [   ]   0.5 [   ]

11.0 [   ]   17.0 [   ]   21.0 [   ]   35.0 [   ]

(3) What is 75% of each number?

12.0 [   ]   8.0 [   ]   6.0 [   ]   24.0 [   ]

36.0 [   ]   16.0 [   ]   22.0 [   ]   14.0 [   ]

Time filler:
Do you know how much you weigh to the nearest kilogram? Step on some scales and find out. Then work out 50%, 0.25, 10% and 0.4 of your weight.

(4) Write the answers.

How long is 25% of 1 hour?

What weight is 45% of 10 kg?

What length is seven-tenths ($\frac{7}{10}$) of 12.5 m?

What distance is 30% of 6 km?

How much is 75% of £12?

What distance is 65% of 200 km?

How much is 30% more than £5?   £5

What distance is 15% more than 2 km?

Decrease 60 m by 20%.

Decrease £300 by 15%.

Subtraction 1

Are you ready to take away?
Subtraction is the opposite of addition.

(1) Write the answers.

$8.0 - 0.5 =$ [ ]

$9.9 - 7.5 =$ [ ]

$4.0 - 0.3 =$ [ ]

$3.0 - 0.2 =$ [ ]

$5.6 - 2.1 =$ [ ]

$7.0 - 0.9 =$ [ ]

$6.2 - 1.1 =$ [ ]

$7.8 - 5.3 =$ [ ]

$9.4 - 3.4 =$ [ ]

$9.5 - 3.2 =$ [ ]

$9.4 - 6.4 =$ [ ]

$7.8 - 5.6 =$ [ ]

$15.6 - 9.2 =$ [ ]

$12.4 - 7.2 =$ [ ]

$10.2 - 8.7 =$ [ ]

$13.8 - 7.9 =$ [ ]

$14.5 - 8.3 =$ [ ]

$10.6 - 3.5 =$ [ ]

$12.8 - 0.9 =$ [ ]

$16.5 - 12.7 =$ [ ]

$28.9 - 26.3 =$ [ ]

$18.6 - 13.4 =$ [ ]

$29.3 - 17.5 =$ [ ]

$24.7 - 11.9 =$ [ ]

Time filler:
Can you do these subtraction sums
in your head?
5.5 – 4.5
7.3 – 4.9
13.61 – 3.01
Are they trickier or easier than addition sums?

(2) Mitesh is 140.5 cm tall and Marc is 136.6 cm
tall. What is the difference in their heights?

....

(3) Work out these subtraction sums.

8.0 – 4.6	6.7 – 3.9	4.3 – 2.8	9.6 – 4.2	5.8 – 1.4

6.43 – 3.29	9.28 – 4.35	6.06 – 2.84	3.0 – 0.8	12.0 – 9.4

8.341 – 2.634	5.078 – 2.563	9.06 –1.99	4.5 – 3.7	7.0 – 2.9

16.70 – 8.45	14.99 – 11.22	24.62 – 17.54	41.07 – 8.41	12.41 – 8.53

Subtraction 2

Now try some harder subtraction sums. Do not forget to add the symbols for units and money to your answers to questions 2–7.

① Write the answers.

5.347	8.231	7.453	2.951	6.523
− 3.200	− 7.003	− 4.560	− 1.460	− 0.692

12.949	78.623	52.070	27.511	69.653
− 4.480	− 29.860	− 14.000	− 13.700	− 5.170

23.000	85.000	42.000	78.000	35.000
− 7.260	− 43.410	− 18.244	− 42.568	− 17.622

34.060	49.768	23.453	55.172	18.643
− 18.040	− 26.769	− 15.564	− 38.081	− 11.931

10.000	20.000	30.000	40.000	60.000
− 4.560	− 17.641	− 20.888	− 27.135	− 34.259

Time filler:
Try this extra devilish decimal question.
Which answer gives the greater
decimal number, 44.362 minus
27.731 or 33.767 minus 17.137?

(2) Answer these questions.

Decrease 4.7 cm by 3.8 cm. [ ]

What is £12 minus £3.48? [ ]

(3) Decrease each length by 0.36 m.

　　5 m　　　　　　　　　4.8 m　　　　　　　　　3.1 m
　[ ]　　　　　　　　[ ]　　　　　　　　[ ]

(4) A path was 7.82 m long. 1.45 m of it was
grassed over. What is the length of the path now?

[ ]

(5) Billy had £42.70 but he spent £6.50.
How much money does Billy have now? [ ]

(6) Middle Brook Street was 5.85 m wide.
A new brick wall reduced the width
by 0.68 m. How wide is the street now?

[ ]

(7) Sandy takes £10.00 out of the bank
and then gives 75 p to charity.
How much money is Sandy left with? [ ]

Beat the clock 2

Work steadily through these questions.
Do not rush, or you'll make mistakes.
Keep calm and go!

Work out each sum and then write the answer.

(1) $5.7 + 3.4 =$ ____   (2) $3.8 + 2.1 =$ ____   (3) $6.1 + 4.5 =$ ____

(4) $7.6 + 5.3 =$ ____   (5) $6.4 + 3.6 =$ ____   (6) $7.1 + 1.9 =$ ____

(7) $5.5 + 3.5 =$ ____   (8) $7.2 + 0.8 =$ ____   (9) $5.6 + 5.6 =$ ____

(10) $7.3 + 6.8 =$ ____   (11) $2.9 + 4.6 =$ ____   (12) $3.8 + 2.8 =$ ____

(13) $2.6 + 3.9 =$ ____   (14) $8.0 + 2.9 =$ ____   (15) $1.3 + 4.8 =$ ____

(16) $0.9 + 0.8 =$ ____   (17) $2.3 + 2.8 =$ ____   (18) $8.8 + 3.9 =$ ____

Work out these slightly harder sums.

(19) $6.34 + 1.06 =$ ____   (20) $7.06 + 3.4 =$ ____

(21) $0.65 + 0.35 =$ ____   (22) $2.06 + 1.04 =$ ____

(23) $3.33 + 4.44 =$ ____   (24) $4.59 + 6.02 =$ ____

(25) $8.05 + 4.89 =$ ____   (26) $7.77 + 0.65 =$ ____

(27) $1.58 + 7.63 =$ ____   (28) $6.63 + 5.09 =$ ____

Time filler:
How did you do? Divide your score by 58 (the number of questions) to give you a decimal amount (to no more than two decimal places). Now work out your score as a percentage.

Work out these sums.

(29) $5.0 - 0.2 =$ ☐

(30) $8.0 - 2.3 =$ ☐

(31) $6.0 - 4.8 =$ ☐

(32) $12.5 - 3.5 =$ ☐

(33) $6.4 - 3.2 =$ ☐

(34) $8.9 - 2.1 =$ ☐

(35) $10.6 - 3.5 =$ ☐

(36) $5.1 - 4.0 =$ ☐

(37) $6.8 - 0.8 =$ ☐

(38) $20.0 - 6.3 =$ ☐

(39) $5.3 - 4.2 =$ ☐

(40) $7.7 - 5.5 =$ ☐

Work out each percentage.

(41) 25% of £5 ☐

(42) 75% of £16 ☐

(43) 50% of £9.50 ☐

(44) 20% of £4 ☐

(45) 60% of 3 m ☐

(46) 25% of £0.84 ☐

(47) 10% of 1.2 m ☐

(48) 10% of £3.20 ☐

(49) 65% of £3 ☐

Write each percentage in its decimal form.

(50) 50% ☐

(51) 10% ☐

(52) 70% ☐

(53) 15% ☐

(54) 5% ☐

(55) 45% ☐

(56) 90% ☐

(57) 34% ☐

(58) 1% ☐

Multiplication 1

When we multiply a decimal by 10, the numbers move around the decimal point one place to the left. Can you see what happens when we multiply by 100 and 1 000?

(1) Multiply each number by 10.

5.0 [ ]	7.5 [ ]	8.6 [ ]	0.3 [ ]
4.2 [ ]	0.8 [ ]	7.1 [ ]	5.7 [ ]
7.44 [ ]	9.25 [ ]	3.09 [ ]	5.12 [ ]
3.17 [ ]	0.71 [ ]	8.54 [ ]	0.89 [ ]
2.645 [ ]	7.321 [ ]	76.342 [ ]	41.545 [ ]

(2) Multiply each number by 100.

3.4 [ ]	6.8 [ ]	7.1 [ ]	5.2 [ ]
6.0 [ ]	2.7 [ ]	9.9 [ ]	1.01 [ ]
8.27 [ ]	4.86 [ ]	12.7 [ ]	13.1 [ ]
5.887 [ ]	5.854 [ ]	34.22 [ ]	75.734 [ ]
43.882 [ ]	33.297 [ ]	423.67 [ ]	123.78 [ ]

Time filler:
Here are a few, slightly trickier, extra questions.
4.4 x 20
8.25 x 300
12.74 x 4 000
How did you go about working them out?

(3) Multiply each number by 1 000.

5.6 [   ]   7.1 [   ]   9.6 [   ]   4.0 [   ]

4.3 [   ]   9.2 [   ]   8.1 [   ]   6.8 [   ]

8.3 [   ]   0.001 [   ]   0.07 [   ]   53.999 [   ]

25.19 [   ]   32.132 [   ]   54.67 [   ]   729.7 [   ]

403.2 [   ]   341.56 [   ]   432.11 [   ]   345.678 [   ]

(4) Write the answers.

320.006 x 10 [   ]   32.143 x 100 [   ]

29.15 x 1 000 [   ]   201.12 x 10 [   ]

17.487 x 1 000 [   ]   56.195 x 100 [   ]

121.165 x 100 [   ]   782.01 x 1 000 [   ]

812.84 x 100 [   ]   297.49 x 1 000 [   ]

253.786 x 10 [   ]   723.707 x 10 [   ]

Division and rounding 1

When we divide a decimal number by 10, the numbers move around the decimal point one place to the right.

(1) What is the place value of 7 in each of these numbers?

2.07	17.63	24.897	315.74
....	....	....	....

7.12	12.37	70.139	29.871
....	....	....	....

(2) Divide each number by 10.

0.07 [ ]   80.0 [ ]   83.86 [ ]   132.678 [ ]

24.8 [ ]   63.96 [ ]   4.331 [ ]   87.2 [ ]

18.4 [ ]   79.12 [ ]   5.211 [ ]   325.986 [ ]

(3) Divide each number by 100.

603.4 [ ]   720.05 [ ]   3 300.8 [ ]   200.005 [ ]

65.2 [ ]   7 324.45 [ ]   723.966 [ ]   53.06 [ ]

6.45 [ ]   7.83 [ ]   34.32 [ ]   8.64 [ ]

(4) Divide each number by 1 000.

6.3 [   ]   73.85 [   ]   923.357 [   ]   1 854.6 [   ]

0.4 [   ]   18.0 [   ]   75.94 [   ]   50.67 [   ]

(5) At the zoo, Eliza the Elephant weighs 3 750 kg. Billy the Bear is
0.1 (one-tenth), Chai the Cheetah is 0.01 (one-hundredth) and
Polly the Penguin is 0.001 (one-thousandth) of Eliza's weight.
How much does each animal weigh?

Chai the Cheetah   Polly the Penguin   Billy the Bear
[   ]   [   ]   [   ]

(6) Round each of these numbers to the nearest whole number.

66.67 [   ]   3.52 [   ]   253.91 [   ]   504.54 [   ]

25.35 [   ]   4.15 [   ]   621.32 [   ]   698.35 [   ]

48.01 [   ]   3.89 [   ]   481.69 [   ]   523.78 [   ]

Multiplication 2

Multiplication sums can be written
out in horizontal and vertical forms.
Which way do you prefer?

① Write the answers.

4.2 x 6 = [   ]   2.6 x 8 = [   ]   3.1 x 2 = [   ]

5.9 x 6 = [   ]   9.6 x 8 = [   ]   1.8 x 9 = [   ]

3.8 x 7 = [   ]   6.6 x 4 = [   ]   2.9 x 8 = [   ]

4.7 x 9 = [   ]   5.98 x 5 = [   ]   7.13 x 6 = [   ]

8.15 x 7 = [   ]   3.65 x 4 = [   ]   9.64 x 2 = [   ]

4.56 x 3 = [   ]   8.24 x 2 = [   ]   9.66 x 4 = [   ]

5.69 x 3 = [   ]   8.64 x 7 = [   ]   7.04 x 5 = [   ]

3.08 x 9 = [   ]   7.68 x 6 = [   ]   8.98 x 9 = [   ]

0.65 x 5 = [   ]   1.06 x 7 = [   ]   6.74 x 7 = [   ]

9.81 x 7 = [   ]   8.07 x 8 = [   ]   9.36 x 4 = [   ]

8.05 x 3 = [   ]   1.09 x 6 = [   ]   9.99 x 5 = [   ]

Time filler:
Make up ten more sums in which decimal numbers are multiplied by whole numbers. Challenge your mum or dad and other members of your family to see who can work them out the fastest.

(2) Work out these multiplication sums.

```
    6.23          7.98          8.56          2.66
x     12      x     18      x     24      x     31
  ...........    ...........    ...........    ...........


    4.07          3.82          9.27          6.07
x     52      x     68      x     42      x     64
  ...........    ...........    ...........    ...........


    9.99          5.08          1.92          4.15
x     85      x     59      x     13      x     16
  ...........    ...........    ...........    ...........


    7.19          1.39          2.81          7.75
x     19      x     14      x     37      x     45
  ...........    ...........    ...........    ...........
```

(3) Simone gets £3.55 as pocket money every week, whereas Charlie gets £16.50 each month. Who gets the most in a year?

Division

You'll be a whizz at dividing decimal numbers when you've worked through these sums. Are you ready?

① Write the answers.

6.4 ÷ 8 = [   ]   9.6 ÷ 8 = [   ]   7.2 ÷ 9 = [   ]

0.4 ÷ 4 = [   ]   1.7 ÷ 10 = [   ]   0.3 ÷ 10 = [   ]

4.9 ÷ 7 = [   ]   0.36 ÷ 2 = [   ]   0.72 ÷ 12 = [   ]

4.2 ÷ 10 = [   ]   0.48 ÷ 6 = [   ]   0.36 ÷ 4 = [   ]

0.75 ÷ 5 = [   ]   1.08 ÷ 9 = [   ]   1.21 ÷ 11 = [   ]

0.54 ÷ 6 = [   ]   7.28 ÷ 8 = [   ]   8.19 ÷ 9 = [   ]

4.97 ÷ 7 = [   ]   2.46 ÷ 6 = [   ]   4.84 ÷ 4 = [   ]

② Emily, Tom and Sky have a jumble sale and make £152.25. The money is divided equally between five charities. How much does each charity receive?

Time filler:
Try these two extra questions. Katya has £16.92 and wants to divide it equally between four friends. How much does each friend get? She also has 1.32 l of fizzy water and wants to pour it into three glasses in equal amounts. How much water should each glass have?

(3) Write the answers.

$4.32 \div 9 =$ ☐ $13.8 \div 6 =$ ☐ $27.3 \div 7 =$ ☐

$16.3 \div 5 =$ ☐ $32.8 \div 4 =$ ☐ $77.4 \div 9 =$ ☐

$64.6 \div 8 =$ ☐ $48.1 \div 5 =$ ☐ $81.9 \div 9 =$ ☐

$87.5 \div 7 =$ ☐ $29.7 \div 4 =$ ☐ $46.8 \div 4 =$ ☐

$89.7 \div 3 =$ ☐ $93.5 \div 2 =$ ☐ $69.3 \div 3 =$ ☐

$88.4 \div 4 =$ ☐ $12.99 \div 6 =$ ☐ $16.56 \div 8 =$ ☐

$28.15 \div 5 =$ ☐ $22.76 \div 4 =$ ☐ $39.12 \div 3 =$ ☐

$53.92 \div 8 =$ ☐ $63.27 \div 9 =$ ☐ $61.12 \div 8 =$ ☐

$53.12 \div 8 =$ ☐ $76.44 \div 6 =$ ☐ $72.36 \div 4 =$ ☐

$75.45 \div 5 =$ ☐ $72.24 \div 6 =$ ☐ $60.41 \div 10 =$ ☐

$80.15 \div 7 =$ ☐ $102.2 \div 7 =$ ☐ $104.8 \div 2 =$ ☐

Division and rounding 2

After you've done a few of these questions, use a calculator to help you with the rest.

1 Work out each division and round the answer to the nearest penny.

£7 ÷ 3	£15 ÷ 7	£31 ÷ 5	£47 ÷ 3

£18.50 ÷ 3	£2.43 ÷ 6	£7.42 ÷ 9	£7.32 ÷ 4

£0.75 ÷ 4	£1.50 ÷ 7	£3 ÷ 9	£2.99 ÷ 4

2 Work out each division and round the answer to the nearest centimetre. (**Hint:** 100 cm = 1 m)

9 m ÷ 7	16 m ÷ 6	45 m ÷ 4	69 m ÷ 2

7 m ÷ 3	26 m ÷ 4	69 m ÷ 5	72 m ÷ 7

3.6 m ÷ 5	4.28 m ÷ 3	12.65 m ÷ 6	7.4 m ÷ 3

12.9 m ÷ 8	8.12 m ÷ 5	18.8 m ÷ 6	25.6 m ÷ 7

Time filler:
Find a recipe for a cake in a book. Imagine that you need just half the amount of each ingredient. Work out the new amounts of flour, sugar, etc. Now imagine you need just one-third of the original amounts. Again, work out the quantities you now need.

(3) Work out each division and round the answer to the nearest gram.
(Hint: 1 000 g = 1 kg)

4 kg ÷ 6	19 kg ÷ 9	23 kg ÷ 12	12 kg ÷ 7

4.7 kg ÷ 6	11.9 kg ÷ 9	18.4 kg ÷ 7	16.9 kg ÷ 3

(4) Work out each division and round the answer to the nearest metre.
(Hint: 1 000 m = 1 km)

2 km ÷ 3	17 km ÷ 8	38 km ÷ 6	33 km ÷ 5

1.78 km ÷ 4	2.06 km ÷ 9	3.63 km ÷ 5	20.4 km ÷ 7

(5) Work out each division and round the answer to the nearest millilitre.
(Hint: 1 000 ml = 1 l)

8 l ÷ 6	13 l ÷ 4	40 l ÷ 7	46 l ÷ 8

23 l ÷ 9	43 l ÷ 5	62 l ÷ 3	17 l ÷ 8

Division and rounding 3

Again, after you've got the hang of these, use a calculator to speed things up. Don't forget to add the symbols for units and money.

1 Work out each answer and round to the nearest pound.

$£17.89 ÷ 3$

$£26.50 ÷ 4$

$£30 ÷ 7$

$£37.15 ÷ 6$

$£275 ÷ 3$

$£723 ÷ 6$

$£26 ÷ 6$

$£295 ÷ 4$

2 Work out each answer and round to the nearest metre.

$34.8\,m ÷ 7$

$41.9\,m ÷ 7$

$60.34\,m ÷ 4$

$28.4\,m ÷ 3$

$2\,364\,m ÷ 7$

$406\,m ÷ 14$

$3\,186\,m ÷ 12$

$5\,123\,m ÷ 11$

3 Work out each answer and round to the nearest centimetre.

$253\,cm ÷ 7$

$4.12\,m ÷ 7$

$372\,cm ÷ 5$

$789\,cm ÷ 7$

$89\,cm ÷ 3$

$1.42\,m ÷ 7$

$56.86\,cm ÷ 4$

$14.19\,cm ÷ 5$

Time filler:
Make up ten of your own division sums that split up money, weights, volumes and lengths into equal quantities. Work them out yourself and then test them on a member of your family.

4 Work out each division and round to the nearest gram.

43 g ÷ 2   317 g ÷ 6   500 g ÷ 6

534 g ÷ 7   2.5 kg ÷ 9   890 g ÷ 12

5 Work out each division and round to the nearest penny. Answer in pounds.

£2 ÷ 3   £53.60 ÷ 7   £120 ÷ 11   £28.30 ÷ 9

£85.62 ÷ 4   £49.12 ÷ 6   £59.52 ÷ 3   £72.12 ÷ 8

6 Work out each division and round to the nearest litre.

582 l ÷ 5   20.16 l ÷ 3   324 l ÷ 6   429 l ÷ 7

456 l ÷ 5   63.85 l ÷ 3   10.02 l ÷ 6   256 l ÷ 7

Decimals and percentages 1

Remember: all percentages have a decimal equivalent. For example: 75% is the same as 0.75.

1 What is 70% of each amount?

£6	£23	6.5 m	37 m

2 Write each decimal as its percentage equivalent.

0.75	0.45	0.333	0.125

0.01	0.9	0.375	0.3

3 Write each percentage in its decimal form.

55%	25%	12.5%	5%

65%	40%	80%	95%

4 What is 35% of each amount?

6 m	4 km	£12	7 m

Time filler:
Here's an extra question. Which amount of money is bigger, 15% of £5 or 90% of 80 p?

(5) What is 5% of each amount?

£16	200 m	£4.60	60 m

(6) What percentage of 200 is each of the following?

50	10	75	150

(7) What percentage of 5 m is each of the following?

50 cm	20 cm	25 cm	2 m

(8) What percentage of £5 is each of the following?

£1	£3	£4.50	10 p

(9) What percentage of 150 is each of the following?

30	15	45	90

Decimals and percentages 2

Make sure you read each question very carefully, so you know what exactly is being asked for. Are you ready?

① A motorway was originally 40 km long but has had its length increased to 60 km. By what percentage has the motorway increased in length?

> ....

② David usually receives £5 pocket money per week, but on his tenth birthday he had the amount raised by 10%. How much pocket money will David receive now?

> ....

③ Sean measured himself on his ninth birthday and was 120 cm tall. On his tenth birthday, he measured himself again and this time he was 144 cm tall. By what percentage has Sean grown?

> ....

④ A container carries 2 000 new television sets. When it was opened, 0.05 of the televisions were broken. How many television sets have not been broken?

> .... television sets

⑤ Emmie usually spends £80 a week on food shopping. Before Christmas, she increased this amount by 0.25. How much money will Emmie spend now?

> ....

Time filler:
What percentage of your family are male? What percentage are female? What percentage of your family are children? And what percentage are adults?

(6) Victoria sends 500 texts per month. While on holiday this number decreases by 70%. How many texts does Victoria send while on holiday?

.... texts

(7) A television programme lasts for one hour, but 0.125 of this time is taken up by advertisements. How long is the programme without the advertisements?

....

(8) What percentage of £1 000 is £50?

....

(9) The area of a football pitch in a stadium is 8 000 m². After alterations, the area is reduced by 15%. What is the new area of the pitch?

....

(10) An amount of money is increased by 35% and is now £27. How much was the amount before the increase?

....

Estimation and rounding

Round up or down decimal numbers
when estimating the multiplication
sums on this page.

(1) Round each amount to the nearest 10 pounds.

£12 753   £27 056   £70 000.24   £38 005.18

(2) Round each amount to the nearest 100 pounds.

£51   £62 348   £92 062   £72 858

(3) Estimate the answers.

10.18 x 12   42.7 x 15   0.23 x 49   37.1 x 18

1.66 x 6   4.94 x 9   56 x 0.8   7.9 x 12

650 x 0.6   412 x 0.8   1 329 x 0.2   2 153 x 0.5

6.82 x 7   2.19 x 8   37 x 0.9   56 x 1.8

Time filler:
Why do we have different units of lengths and weights? Why is it easier to measure the length of small things in centimetres, rather than in metres and kilometres? Why is it easier to use grams to weigh ingredients in a recipe, rather than kilograms and tonnes? Discuss the reasons with your parents.

(4) Round each amount to nearest kilogram.

12 481 g   26 099 g   245 034 g   45 108 g

(5) Round each distance to the nearest kilometre.

6 783 m   15 480 m   274 199 m   482 715 m

(6) The cost of a mobile phone is £480. During a sale, it is sold for £360. By what percentage has the price been reduced?

(7) Copper piping is sold in lengths of 2.35 m. A plumber needs 15 m of piping. How many lengths will he need?

.... lengths

(8) Petrol costs £1.36 per litre. How many whole litres of petrol can be bought for £20?

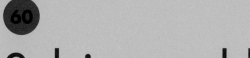

Solving problems 1

These problems will test the maths skills
you've already covered in this book.
See how you get on.

① Which is larger, 30% of £20 or 15% of £50?

....

What is the difference between the two amounts?

② Which is longer, 20% of 180 m or 45% of 400 m?

....

What is the difference between the two lengths?

③ Which weighs more, 18% of 3 kg or 12% of 4 kg?

....

What is the difference between the weights?

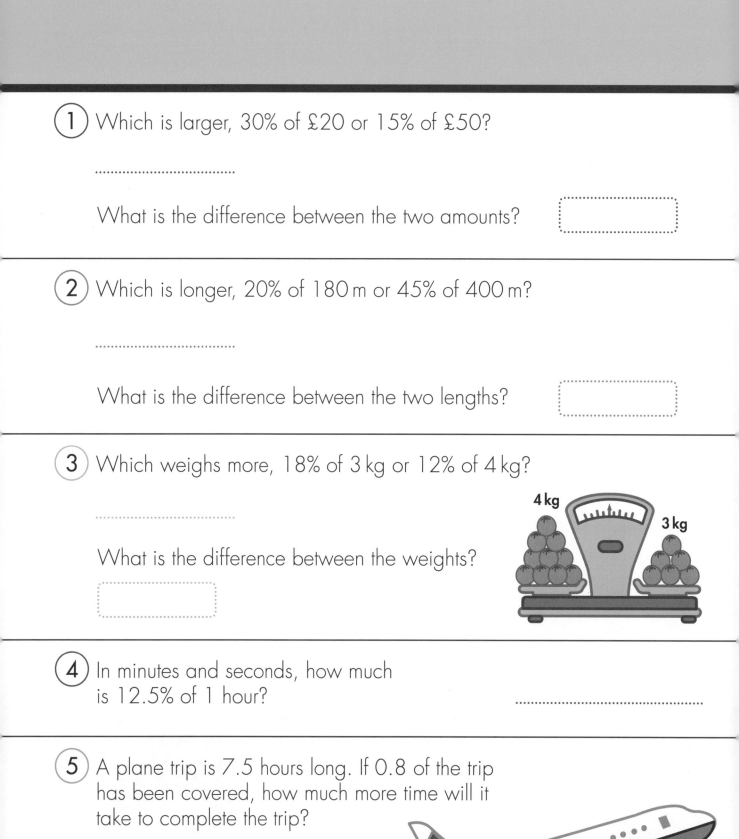

④ In minutes and seconds, how much
is 12.5% of 1 hour?

....

⑤ A plane trip is 7.5 hours long. If 0.8 of the trip
has been covered, how much more time will it
take to complete the trip?

Time filler:
Are you hungry for another problem? Lizzie made a fruitcake and divided it into nine equal slices. Scott ate two slices and Craig ate five! What percentage of the cake did Scott eat and what percentage did Craig eat? Round your answers to the nearest percent.

6) Divide 6% of 300 by 0.4 of 30.

7) Susan gives 10% of her salary to charity each month. If Susan is paid £1 780 each month, how much will she give to charity each year?

£100
£100

8) What amount is...

... 15% less than £500?

... 45% more than £5 000?

9) What percentage of...

... 84 is 21?

... 400 is 20?

10) Fill in the boxes.

Reduce 4 km by 2%.

Increase 6 kg by 3.5%.

Solving problems 2

Read each question slowly and think
carefully. Rushing will increase the
risk of making mistakes.

1 What number is 60% more than each of these?

180   340   750

[ ]   [ ]   [ ]

2 What is 0.01 of each amount? Write your answers in pounds.

£12   £250   £800

[ ]   [ ]   [ ]

3 When a number is multiplied by 1.78,
the result is 21.36. What is the number?   [ ]

4 Fill in the boxes.

40% of a number is 12. What is the number?   [ ]

36% of a number is 72. What is the number?   [ ]

70% of a number is 98. What is the number?   [ ]

0.7 of a number is 14. What is the number?   [ ]

0.3 of a number is 5.4. What is the number?   [ ]

0.2 of a number is 2. What is the number?   [ ]

Time filler:
Try this extra problem: Grandma Jones gives her three grandchildren £8 to share. Charlie, the oldest, takes 45% of the money, Joanna, in the middle, takes 35% and Alexander, the youngest, is left with 20%. How much money does each receive?

(5) If a van travels at an average speed of 34.8 mph, how far will it travel in 5 hours?

(6) Work out the answers.

If 64 is 0.8 of a number, what is the number?

What is 0.72 of 119?

If 35 is 0.5 of a number, what is the number?

What is 0.29 of 520?

(7) Nola usually scores 40 out of 50 in maths tests. After some special revision, her score goes up by 15%. What is Nola's score now?

(8) At the beginning of the year, a gold coin cost £450 but by the end of the year, its cost went up by 25%. What is its cost at the end of the year?

£100

Beat the clock 3

If you're not happy with your score or time, try this quick-fire round again the next day to see if you can improve it.

Multiply each number by 10.

(1)   7.5 [ ]   (2)   16.8 [ ]   (3)   0.03 [ ]

Multiply each number by 100.

(4)   7.09 [ ]   (5)   24.05 [ ]   (6)   3.06 [ ]

Multiply each number by 1 000.

(7)   0.5 [ ]   (8)   3.88 [ ]   (9)   100.1 [ ]

Divide each number by 10.

(10)   4.6 [ ]   (11)   60.1 [ ]   (12)   103.0 [ ]

Divide each number by 100.

(13)   16.0 [ ]   (14)   4 250 [ ]   (15)   30.05 [ ]

Divide each number by 1 000.

(16)   43 967 [ ]   (17)   132 900 [ ]   (18)   78 519 [ ]

Time filler:
Now you're an expert on decimal numbers! If you want more practice, see if you can write your own mini "Beat the clock" page, with a mixture of 20 addition, subtraction, multiplication and division sums.

Round each number to two decimal places.

(19) 4.893 [ ]   (20) 6.888 [ ]   (21) 8.005 [ ]

(22) 17.006 [ ]   (23) 31.416 [ ]   (24) 24.435 [ ]

(25) 65.007 [ ]   (26) 80.005 [ ]   (27) 236.991 [ ]

Round each number to three decimal places.

(28) 2.8745 [ ]   (29) 0.5555 [ ]   (30) 1.0007 [ ]

(31) 52.0502 [ ]   (32) 6.3512 [ ]   (33) 28.6891 [ ]

Quickly write the answers.

(34) 2 x 0.6 [ ]   (35) 12 x 1.2 [ ]   (36) 16 x 0.3 [ ]

(37) 2.7 x 5 [ ]   (38) 0.2 x 75 [ ]   (39) 0.6 x 500 [ ]

(40) 3.8 x 4 [ ]   (41) 2.8 x 0.5 [ ]   (42) 0.3 x 0.3 [ ]

(43) 24 x 0.25 [ ]   (44) 0.7 x 0.4 [ ]   (45) 30% of 60 [ ]

(46) 25% of 1 [ ]   (47) 45% of 400 [ ]   (48) 300 x 0.75 [ ]

Answers:

04–05 Equivalents 1
06–07 Equivalents 2

4

① Shade in 0.5 of each shape.

② Shade in 0.25 of each shape.

③ Shade in 0.75 of each shape.

④ Write each decimal as a fraction.

$0.5\ \frac{1}{2}$ $0.25\ \frac{1}{4}$ $0.75\ \frac{3}{4}$

⑤ Draw lines linking each decimal amount to the shape with the equivalent area shaded.

0.5
0.25
0.75

⑥ What decimal amount of each shape has been shaded?

0.75   0.25
0.5   0.5
0.25   0.5
0.5   0.5

⑦ Write the corresponding decimal for each shaded portion.

0.5
0.75

Your child should quickly recognise how much of each shape is shaded, including more complex shapes or places where six out of eight parts are shaded.

Your child should immediately translate $\frac{6}{8}$ to $\frac{3}{4}$, for example, and then to 0.75 without being reminded.

6

① Write each fraction as a decimal.

$\frac{1}{10}$ 0.1 $\frac{1}{100}$ 0.01 $\frac{3}{10}$ 0.3 $\frac{7}{100}$ 0.07

$\frac{6}{10}$ 0.6 $\frac{9}{10}$ 0.9 $\frac{3}{100}$ 0.03 $\frac{9}{100}$ 0.09

$\frac{6}{100}$ 0.06 $\frac{5}{10}$ 0.5 $\frac{8}{100}$ 0.08 $\frac{2}{100}$ 0.02

$\frac{2}{10}$ 0.2 $\frac{4}{10}$ 0.4 $\frac{7}{10}$ 0.7 $\frac{4}{100}$ 0.04

$\frac{12}{10}$ 1.2 $\frac{68}{100}$ 0.68 $\frac{23}{100}$ 0.23 $\frac{10}{100}$ 0.1

$\frac{45}{10}$ 4.5 $\frac{32}{100}$ 0.32 $\frac{51}{10}$ 5.1 $\frac{97}{100}$ 0.97

$\frac{61}{100}$ 0.61 $\frac{18}{10}$ 1.8 $\frac{33}{10}$ 3.3 $\frac{75}{100}$ 0.75

$\frac{28}{10}$ 2.8 $\frac{87}{10}$ 8.7 $\frac{66}{100}$ 0.66 $\frac{22}{100}$ 0.22

$\frac{52}{100}$ 0.52 $\frac{19}{10}$ 1.9 $\frac{73}{100}$ 0.73 $\frac{92}{10}$ 9.2

② Write each decimal as a fraction.

$0.08\ \frac{8}{100}$ $0.15\ \frac{15}{100}$ $0.06\ \frac{6}{100}$ $0.27\ \frac{27}{100}$ $0.9\ \frac{9}{10}$

$0.34\ \frac{34}{100}$ $0.57\ \frac{57}{100}$ $0.05\ \frac{5}{100}$ $0.97\ \frac{97}{100}$ $0.02\ \frac{2}{100}$

$0.62\ \frac{62}{100}$ $0.48\ \frac{48}{100}$ $0.23\ \frac{23}{100}$ $0.71\ \frac{71}{100}$ $0.6\ \frac{6}{10}$

$0.01\ \frac{1}{100}$ $0.1\ \frac{1}{10}$ $0.5\ \frac{5}{10}$ $0.68\ \frac{68}{100}$ $0.7\ \frac{7}{10}$

$0.25\ \frac{25}{100}$ $0.75\ \frac{75}{100}$ $0.3\ \frac{3}{10}$ $0.03\ \frac{3}{100}$ $0.8\ \frac{8}{10}$

In some of the answers, it may be possible to simplify the solution. For example, $\frac{5}{10}$ can be simplified to $\frac{1}{2}$. Your child will be learning to simplify fractions at school at the same time as this work, so expect some of these answers to be in a simplified form.

Answers:

08–09 Dividing by 10 and 100
10–11 Rounding decimals

8

① Write whether 1 is in the ten, unit, tenth or hundredth place in these numbers.

1.0	0.1	0.01	2.1	32.01
Unit	Tenth	Hundredth	Tenth	Hundredth

4.12	21.8	7.1	1.2	10.6
Tenth	Unit	Tenth	Unit	Ten

② Suki has a total of £13.68 in her piggy bank. Which part of that number is the unit place and which is the tenth place?

Unit [3]

Tenth [6]

③ Divide each number by 10 and write the answer in the decimal form.

50 [5.0]	4 [0.4]	81 [8.1]	70 [7.0]	25 [2.5]
7 [0.7]	35 [3.5]	60 [6.0]	90 [9.0]	5 [0.5]
15 [1.5]	11 [1.1]	18 [1.8]	20 [2.0]	32 [3.2]

9

④ Divide each number by 100 and write the answer in the decimal form.

78 [0.78]	12 [0.12]	43 [0.43]	9 [0.09]	99 [0.99]
40 [0.4]	5 [0.05]	66 [0.66]	1 [0.01]	50 [0.5]
32 [0.32]	10 [0.1]	70 [0.7]	55 [0.55]	92 [0.92]

⑤ Write whether 5 is in the ten, unit, tenth or hundredth place in these numbers.

56.3	7.05	0.5	5.62	0.05
Ten	Hundredth	Tenth	Unit	Hundredth

15.2	12.5	51.9	20.5	5.78
Unit	Tenth	Ten	Tenth	Unit

⑥ Write whether 8 is in the unit, tenth or hundredth place in these numbers.

7.68	8.6	9.83	12.08	8.43
Hundredth	Unit	Tenth	Hundredth	Unit

4.81	10.8	8.24	6.38	18.5
Tenth	Tenth	Unit	Hundredth	Unit

When working out 40 divided by 10, for example, it is not strictly necessary to write the answer as 4.0. An answer of 4 would be correct, but it is helpful to write the full form so your child becomes used to thinking in the decimal format.

10

① Round each decimal to the nearest whole number.

6.3 [6]	7.6 [8]	9.8 [10]
4.2 [4]	0.5 [1]	24.5 [25]
24.9 [25]	15.5 [16]	15.7 [16]
42.5 [43]	12.1 [12]	49.8 [50]
18.2 [18]	56.4 [56]	79.5 [80]
17.3 [17]	89.5 [90]	57.7 [58]
93.9 [94]	69.9 [70]	87.9 [88]
88.4 [88]	88.5 [89]	88.6 [89]
68.5 [69]	85.6 [86]	65.8 [66]
32.7 [33]	73.3 [73]	88.8 [89]
90.5 [91]	42.6 [43]	59.1 [59]
40.5 [41]	52.5 [53]	73.4 [73]

11

② Round each decimal to the nearest whole unit.

4.5 cm [5 cm]	3.8 m [4 m]	7.1 km [7 km]
56.4 g [56 g]	2.3 kg [2 kg]	12.5 g [13 g]
66.6 m [67 m]	86.5 mm [87 mm]	42.8 kg [43 kg]
47.6 cm [48 cm]	17.3 cm [17 cm]	19.1 km [19 km]
15.5 cm [16 cm]	81.7 mm [82 mm]	23.7 kg [24 kg]
14.2 g [14 g]	56.5 m [57 m]	68.8 km [69 km]
49.2 m [49 m]	35.7 cm [36 cm]	26.6 mm [27 mm]
76.4 m [76 m]	76.5 cm [77 cm]	76.6 mm [77 mm]
67.5 g [68 g]	57.2 kg [57 kg]	57.7 km [58 km]

③ Caleb's favourite book is 21.2 cm wide, 30.5 cm long and 1.9 cm thick. Round these measurements to the nearest centimetre.

[21 cm] [31 cm] [2 cm]

The main stumbling block here is the "halfway" point of 5 where some children are unsure about going "up" or "down". The standard rule is to always go upwards. For example, 76.5 would become 77.

Answers:

12–13 Comparing decimals 1
14–15 Measurements and money

12 **13**

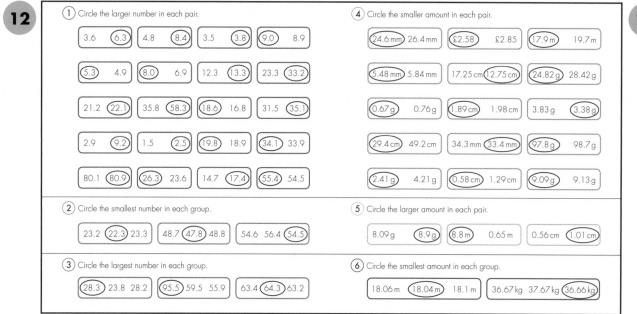

(1) Circle the larger number in each pair.

3.6 (6.3)	4.8 (8.4)	3.5 (3.8)	(9.0) 8.9
(5.3) 4.9	(8.0) 6.9	12.3 (13.3)	23.3 (33.2)
21.2 (22.1)	35.8 (58.3)	(18.6) 16.8	31.5 (35.1)
2.9 (9.2)	1.5 (2.5)	(19.8) 18.9	(34.1) 33.9
80.1 (80.9)	(26.3) 23.6	14.7 (17.4)	(55.4) 54.5

(2) Circle the smallest number in each group.

23.2 (22.3) 23.3   48.7 (47.8) 48.8   54.6 56.4 (54.5)

(3) Circle the largest number in each group.

(28.3) 23.8 28.2   (95.5) 59.5 55.9   63.4 (64.3) 63.2

(4) Circle the smaller amount in each pair.

(24.6 mm) 26.4 mm	(£2.58) £2.85	(17.9 m) 19.7 m
(5.48 mm) 5.84 mm	17.25 cm (12.75 cm)	(24.82 g) 28.42 g
(0.67 g) 0.76 g	(1.89 cm) 1.98 cm	3.83 g (3.38 g)
(29.4 cm) 49.2 cm	34.3 mm (33.4 mm)	(97.8 g) 98.7 g
(2.41 g) 4.21 g	(0.58 cm) 1.29 cm	(9.09 g) 9.13 g

(5) Circle the larger amount in each pair.

8.09 g (8.9 g)   (8.8 m) 0.65 m   0.56 cm (1.01 cm)

(6) Circle the smallest amount in each group.

18.06 m (18.04 m) 18.1 m   36.67 kg 37.67 kg (36.66 kg)

Your child must pay special attention to what is being asked for – larger or smaller. This tests knowledge of place value. Your child should start to "sort" the numbers by looking at the tens column first, followed by the units, tenths and hundredths and then comparing their sizes.

14 **15**

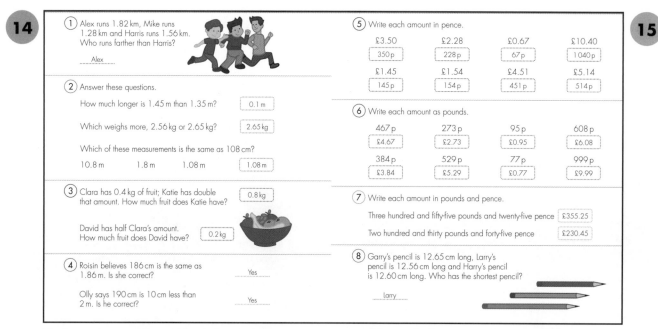

(1) Alex runs 1.82 km, Mike runs 1.28 km and Harris runs 1.56 km. Who runs farther than Harris?

....Alex....

(2) Answer these questions.

How much longer is 1.45 m than 1.35 m?   0.1 m

Which weighs more, 2.56 kg or 2.65 kg?   2.65 kg

Which of these measurements is the same as 108 cm?

10.8 m   1.8 m   1.08 m   1.08 m

(3) Clara has 0.4 kg of fruit; Katie has double that amount. How much fruit does Katie have?   0.8 kg

David has half Clara's amount. How much fruit does David have?   0.2 kg

(4) Roisin believes 186 cm is the same as 1.86 m. Is she correct?   Yes

Olly says 190 cm is 10 cm less than 2 m. Is he correct?   Yes

(5) Write each amount in pence.

£3.50	£2.28	£0.67	£10.40
350 p	228 p	67 p	1040 p
£1.45	£1.54	£4.51	£5.14
145 p	154 p	451 p	514 p

(6) Write each amount as pounds.

467 p	273 p	95 p	608 p
£4.67	£2.73	£0.95	£6.08
384 p	529 p	77 p	999 p
£3.84	£5.29	£0.77	£9.99

(7) Write each amount in pounds and pence.

Three hundred and fifty-five pounds and twenty-five pence   £355.25

Two hundred and thirty pounds and forty-five pence   £230.45

(8) Garry's pencil is 12.65 cm long, Larry's pencil is 12.56 cm long and Harry's pencil is 12.60 cm long. Who has the shortest pencil?

....Larry....

The key to these problems is "unpacking" what operation is needed. Once that is established, the solution should be straightforward. The more practice your child can have with simple "real-life" problems, the better.

Answers:

16–17 Equivalents 3
18–19 Equivalents 4
20–21 Beat the clock 1, see p.80

16 / **17**

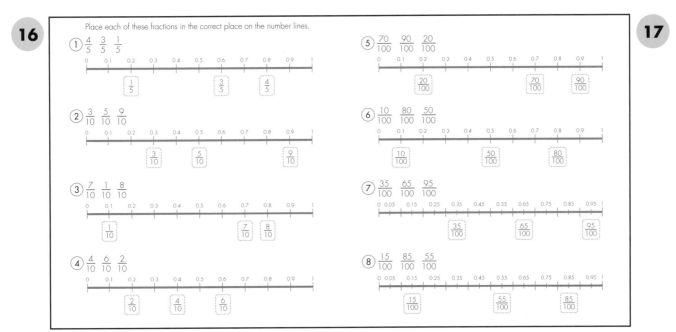

Your child needs to be careful about placing the required fraction on the number line by taking careful note of tenths and hundredths.

18 / **19**

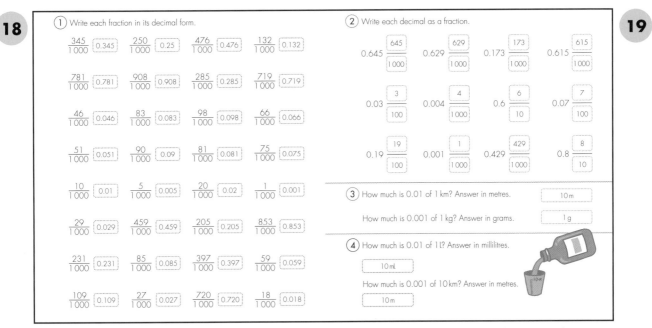

A number such as 0.48 is sometimes shown as just .48, but it is helpful to your child if he or she becomes used to using a fuller format for decimal amounts.

Writing out the decimal form of a fraction, and vice versa, may seem tricky at first. So, the more practice, the better.

Answers:

22–23 Addition 1
24–25 Addition 2

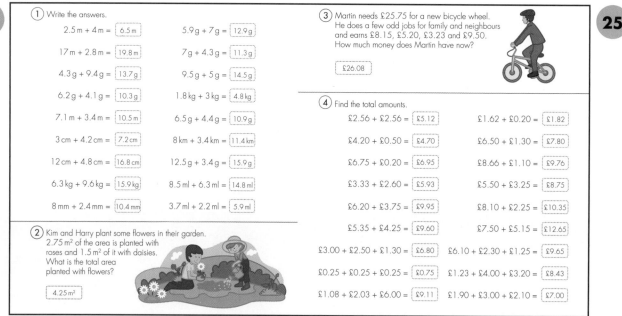

22

① Find the totals.

3 + 1.5 = 4.5	5 + 2.5 = 7.5
8.3 + 4 = 12.3	6.4 + 5 = 11.4
7 + 0.2 = 7.2	1 + 1.4 = 2.4
6.9 + 3 = 9.9	5 + 2.2 = 7.2
7.4 + 3 = 10.4	12.3 + 8 = 20.3
2.4 + 6 = 8.4	4.4 + 6 = 10.4
12 + 8.6 = 20.6	17.4 + 3 = 20.4
18.7 + 6 = 24.7	7.3 + 7 = 14.3
14 + 0.7 = 14.7	24 + 0.3 = 24.3

② On holiday, Richard spent 3 days in France, 0.5 days in Luxembourg, 2.5 days in Belgium and 3.5 days in the Netherlands. How long was Richard's holiday?

9.5 days

23

③ Find the totals.

3 + 4.6 + 2 = 9.6	1.2 + 3 + 5 = 9.2
6 + 8 + 3.5 = 17.5	6 + 4 + 0.1 = 10.1
6.3 + 4 + 4 = 14.3	4.5 + 6 + 3 = 13.5
8 + 3.9 + 3 = 14.9	7.9 + 1 + 3 = 11.9
4.6 + 4 + 6 = 14.6	0.9 + 1 + 7 = 8.9
9.1 + 9 + 2 = 20.1	0.6 + 4 + 5 = 9.6
3.4 + 5 + 6 = 14.4	8 + 9 + 5.4 = 22.4
7 + 6.3 + 4 = 17.3	6.6 + 6 + 6 = 18.6
6 + 4.3 + 12 = 22.3	5.1 + 9 + 3 = 17.1
4.8 + 6 + 9 = 19.8	17 + 3 + 0.2 = 20.2
7 + 2.2 + 8 = 17.2	12 + 7 + 5.9 = 24.9
4 + 7 + 6.9 = 17.9	24 + 8 + 0.8 = 32.8

With these questions, your child needs to recognise the values of each figure, especially the decimals. Although the addition is fairly straightforward, your child needs to be careful when the decimal amount appears first, as in 0.4 + 3, which can be confusing.

24

① Write the answers.

2.5 m + 4 m = 6.5 m	5.9 g + 7 g = 12.9 g
17 m + 2.8 m = 19.8 m	7 g + 4.3 g = 11.3 g
4.3 g + 9.4 g = 13.7 g	9.5 g + 5 g = 14.5 g
6.2 g + 4.1 g = 10.3 g	1.8 kg + 3 kg = 4.8 kg
7.1 m + 3.4 m = 10.5 m	6.5 g + 4.4 g = 10.9 g
3 cm + 4.2 cm = 7.2 cm	8 km + 3.4 km = 11.4 km
12 cm + 4.8 cm = 16.8 cm	12.5 g + 3.4 g = 15.9 g
6.3 kg + 9.6 kg = 15.9 kg	8.5 ml + 6.3 ml = 14.8 ml
8 mm + 2.4 mm = 10.4 mm	3.7 ml + 2.2 ml = 5.9 ml

② Kim and Harry plant some flowers in their garden. 2.75 m² of the area is planted with roses and 1.5 m² of it with daisies. What is the total area planted with flowers?

4.25 m²

25

③ Martin needs £25.75 for a new bicycle wheel. He does a few odd jobs for family and neighbours and earns £8.15, £5.20, £3.23 and £9.50. How much money does Martin have now?

£26.08

④ Find the total amounts.

£2.56 + £2.56 = £5.12	£1.62 + £0.20 = £1.82
£4.20 + £0.50 = £4.70	£6.50 + £1.30 = £7.80
£6.75 + £0.20 = £6.95	£8.66 + £1.10 = £9.76
£3.33 + £2.60 = £5.93	£5.50 + £3.25 = £8.75
£6.20 + £3.75 = £9.95	£8.10 + £2.25 = £10.35
£5.35 + £4.25 = £9.60	£7.50 + £5.15 = £12.65
£3.00 + £2.50 + £1.30 = £6.80	£6.10 + £2.30 + £1.25 = £9.65
£0.25 + £0.25 + £0.25 = £0.75	£1.23 + £4.00 + £3.20 = £8.43
£1.08 + £2.03 + £6.00 = £9.11	£1.90 + £3.00 + £2.10 = £7.00

These questions continue with simple addition, although units are included. Your child should get into the habit of always writing the units. The last questions involve some carrying over and your child needs to be careful.

Answers:

26–27 Comparing decimals 2
28–29 Addition 3

26 / 27

1) Circle the larger number in each pair.

(3.6) 1.9 | (5.86) 5.68 | 7.674 (7.688) | (1.03) 1.003

2) Circle the smaller number in each pair.

(2.05) 2.48 | 3.867 (3.847) | 5.231 (4.999) | (5.051) 5.105

3) Rewrite each row in order, starting with the smallest number.

3.756	3.75	3.675	3.57
3.57	3.675	3.75	3.756

4.086	4.085	4.058	4.068
4.058	4.068	4.085	4.086

12.3	11.9	13.867	11.444
11.444	11.9	12.3	13.867

8.23	3.82	2.83	3.28
2.83	3.28	3.82	8.23

4) Circle the larger amount in each pair.

(6.72 cm) 6.27 cm | 4.88 g (4.91 g) | (6.03 m) 3.6 m

5) Circle the smaller amount in each pair.

(8.326 kg) 8.623 kg | 4.845 km (3.999 km) | 5.123 m (5.104 m)

6) Rewrite each row in order, starting with the largest amount.

4.867 km	4.881 km	6.496 km	4.904 km
6.496 km	4.904 km	4.881 km	4.867 km

18.826 kg	12.978 kg	31.423 kg	31.4 kg
31.423 kg	31.4 kg	18.826 kg	12.978 kg

£7.49	£7.40	£8.00	£7.94
£8.00	£7.94	£7.49	£7.40

£15.67	£18.23	£15.76	£17.78
£18.23	£17.78	£15.76	£15.67

This work will test your child's understanding of place value and he or she will need to take great care when ordering the amounts. Your child needs to look carefully at the number in each position, starting with the largest and then working towards the smallest.

28 / 29

1) Add the numbers.

3.6 + 2.8 = 6.4 | 4.4 + 9.3 = 13.7 | 7.6 + 2.9 = 10.5

6.25 + 4.4 = 10.65 | 4.4 + 18.3 = 22.7 | 7.2 + 11.2 = 18.4

3.71 + 8.81 = 12.52 | 4.55 + 1.25 = 5.8 | 3.05 + 2.05 = 5.1

8.92 + 4.19 = 13.11 | 3.85 + 1.05 = 4.9 | 12.3 + 3.8 = 16.1

6.12 + 2.08 = 8.2 | 13.7 + 2.4 = 16.1 | 29.5 + 6.2 = 35.7

2) Find the totals.

3.0 + 6.1 + 7.3 = 16.4 | 7.3 + 2.4 + 1.6 = 11.3

5.4 + 3.2 + 1.0 = 9.6 | 2.8 + 6.5 + 3.2 = 12.5

6.7 + 3.9 + 4.9 = 15.5 | 8.2 + 5.0 + 3.8 = 17.0

4.9 + 8.8 + 1.4 = 15.1 | 6.5 + 4.5 + 3.5 = 14.5

12.2 + 4.4 + 10.0 = 26.6 | 13.2 + 5.5 + 12.6 = 31.3

3) Work out the answers.

4.6	5.6	7.1	9.3	6.1
+ 3.4	+ 6.8	+ 3.4	+ 1.4	+ 4.8
8.0	12.4	10.5	10.7	10.9

12.8	11.6	15.3	24.7	64.8
+ 6.7	+ 4.7	+ 2.9	+ 3.3	+ 7.4
19.5	16.3	18.2	28.0	72.2

4.63	5.89	1.07	4.36	8.26
+ 1.27	+ 2.33	+ 2.46	+ 1.44	+ 1.74
5.90	8.22	3.53	5.80	10.00

60.34	31.23	56.12	23.99	33.93
+31.47	+14.56	+21.08	+12.01	+83.72
91.81	45.79	77.20	36.00	117.65

4) Each morning, Zara and Kyle walk 0.35 km to the bus stop, travel 3.85 km on the bus and then walk 0.25 km to reach their school. How far is their journey?

4.45 km

Your child should become familiar with simple additions in both horizontal and vertical forms. Some answers are whole numbers, for example, 50. Although writing just the number is acceptable and normal, it is better to have your child write a slightly fuller answer, such as 50.0, as he or she is working with decimals.

Answers:

30–31 Addition 4
32–33 Addition 5

30

① Find the totals.

$3.48 + 5.52 =$ 9.00 $1.09 + 0.91 =$ 2.00

$3.0 + 6.464 =$ 9.464 $4.89 + 2.11 =$ 7.00

$6.042 + 1.1 =$ 7.142 $5.109 + 7.9 =$ 13.009

$5.64 + 2.364 =$ 8.004 $2.34 + 4.001 =$ 6.341

$7.25 + 3.593 =$ 10.843 $7.62 + 3.041 =$ 10.661

② Work out these addition sums.

2.65	1.783	6.20	9.132	2.391
+ 1.46	+2.620	+ 3.88	+1.410	+ 0.129
4.11	4.403	10.08	10.542	2.520
52.60	81.230	56.902	7.008	4.150
+ 8.23	+ 3.284	+6.700	+0.830	+ 1.213
60.83	84.514	63.602	7.838	5.363
23.600	0.600	12.850	4.94	6.403
+ 0.123	+ 3.567	+ 9.006	+ 0.70	+4.892
23.723	4.167	21.856	5.64	11.295

31

③ Answer these questions.

How much is £3.56 plus £2.99?   £6.55

What is 1.56 m added to 1.86 m?   3.42 m

How much is 1.675 km increased by 0.255 km?   1.93 km

What amount is £2.67 more than £12.50?   £15.17

④ A kitchen worktop is made up of two pieces. One piece is 1.645 m long and the other 0.546 m. What will be the length of the whole worktop when the two pieces are joined together?

2.191 m

⑤ What is the total when £2.85 is added to each of these?

£2.69   £5.54   £4.50   £7.35

⑥ Add this group of numbers and write the total.

2.455   7.234   8.167   17.856

Although some sums are written in the horizontal format, your child should be allowed to rewrite the sum in vertical format if he or she prefers. Great care should be taken with all the additions, especially when the numbers have different amounts of decimal figures, as in 2.1 + 32.045.

32

① A car makes three journeys. The first journey is 8.627 km, the second is 9.348 km and the third is 12.450 km. How far does the car travel in total?

30.425 km

② Write the answers.

2.423	1.867	0.655	7.291
+ 1.534	+ 2.427	+ 2.809	+ 0.810
3.957	4.294	3.464	8.101
0.836	2.056	7.340	4.980
+ 6.190	+ 1.006	+ 8.455	+ 2.713
7.026	3.062	15.795	7.693
4.006	3.501	2.956	12.535
+ 1.040	+ 0.660	+ 0.300	+ 6.375
5.046	4.161	3.256	18.910
10.044	12.800	6.834	9.471
2.860	0.640	1.423	1.250
+ 8.009	+ 4.235	+ 0.223	+ 3.089
20.913	17.675	8.480	13.810

33

③ Find the totals.

$4.6 + 3.4 =$ 8.0 $6.6 + 3.9 =$ 10.5

$7.3 + 4.1 =$ 11.4 $7.9 + 2.2 =$ 10.1

$5.6 + 12.8 =$ 18.4 $1.2 + 3.9 =$ 5.1

$3.8 + 4.21 =$ 8.01 $3.45 + 0.45 =$ 3.90

$12.5 + 6.5 =$ 19.0 $4.65 + 0.25 =$ 4.90

$8.22 + 7.33 =$ 15.55 $2.065 + 0.023 =$ 2.088

$1.2 + 3.4 + 2.6 =$ 7.20 $5.6 + 2.3 + 5.3 =$ 13.2

$6.3 + 0.5 + 4.3 =$ 11.1 $7.5 + 4.5 + 3.5 =$ 15.5

$7.1 + 8.2 + 9.3 =$ 24.6 $7.0 + 6.72 + 2.45 =$ 16.17

④ Cressida ran 2.50 km on Monday, 7.01 km on Wednesday and 3.09 km on Saturday. What is the total distance she ran during that week?

12.6 km

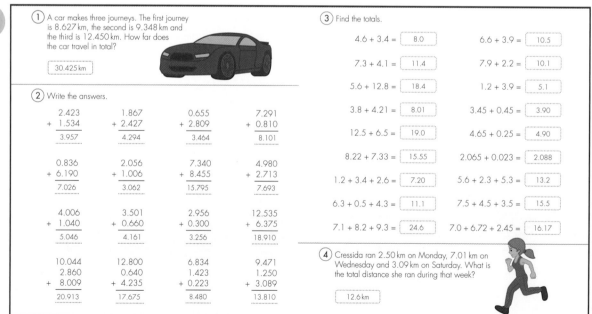

The addition problems are gradually becoming more difficult and your child will need to be very careful with these sums. Your child should become familiar with addition of three numbers.

Answers:

34–35 Decimals, fractions and percentages
36–37 Subtraction 1

34

① What is 25% of each number?

8.4 [2.1]   12.0 [3.0]   6.4 [1.6]   20.4 [5.1]

6.0 [1.5]   9.2 [2.3]   16.8 [4.2]   440.0 [110.0]

② What is 50% of each number?

3.0 [1.5]   7.0 [3.5]   1.2 [0.6]   0.5 [0.25]

11.0 [5.5]   17.0 [8.5]   21.0 [10.5]   35.0 [17.5]

③ What is 75% of each number?

12.0 [9.0]   8.0 [6.0]   6.0 [4.5]   24.0 [18.0]

36.0 [27.0]   16.0 [12.0]   22.0 [16.5]   14.0 [10.5]

35

④ Write the answers.

How long is 25% of 1 hour?   [15 minutes]

What weight is 45% of 10 kg?   [4.5 kg]

What length is seven-tenths ($\frac{7}{10}$) of 12.5 m?   [8.75 m]

What distance is 30% of 6 km?   [1.8 km]

How much is 75% of £12?   [£9]

What distance is 65% of 200 km?   [130 km]

How much is 30% more than £5? **£5**   [£6.50]

What distance is 15% more than 2 km?   [2.3 km]

Decrease 60 m by 20%.   [48 m]

Decrease £300 by 15%.   [£255]

Your child should have simple conversions between decimal amounts and percentages at his or her fingertips. He or she should be able to answer most of these questions in his or her head.

36

① Write the answers.

8.0 − 0.5 = [7.5]   9.9 − 7.5 = [2.4]

4.0 − 0.3 = [3.7]   3.0 − 0.2 = [2.8]

5.6 − 2.1 = [3.5]   7.0 − 0.9 = [6.1]

6.2 − 1.1 = [5.1]   7.8 − 5.3 = [2.5]

9.4 − 3.4 = [6.0]   9.5 − 3.2 = [6.3]

9.4 − 6.4 = [3.0]   7.8 − 5.6 = [2.2]

15.6 − 9.2 = [6.4]   12.4 − 7.2 = [5.2]

10.2 − 8.7 = [1.5]   13.8 − 7.9 = [5.9]

14.5 − 8.3 = [6.2]   10.6 − 3.5 = [7.1]

12.8 − 0.9 = [11.9]   16.5 − 12.7 = [3.8]

28.9 − 26.3 = [2.6]   18.6 − 13.4 = [5.2]

29.3 − 17.5 = [11.8]   24.7 − 11.9 = [12.8]

37

② Mitesh is 140.5 cm tall and Marc is 136.6 cm tall. What is the difference in their heights?

[3.9 cm]

③ Work out these subtraction sums.

8.0	6.7	4.3	9.6	5.8
− 4.6	− 3.9	− 2.8	− 4.2	− 1.4
3.4	2.8	1.5	5.4	4.4

6.43	9.28	6.06	3.0	12.0
− 3.29	− 4.35	− 2.84	− 0.8	− 9.4
3.14	4.93	3.22	2.2	2.6

8.341	5.078	9.06	4.5	7.0
− 2.634	− 2.563	− 1.99	− 3.7	− 2.9
5.707	2.515	7.07	0.8	4.1

16.70	14.99	24.62	41.07	12.41
− 8.45	− 11.22	− 17.54	− 8.41	− 8.53
8.25	3.77	7.08	32.66	3.88

If your child prefers vertical subtraction, let him or her rewrite the sums in that format. While solving subtraction sums, be careful with placing numbers between the columns of numbers.

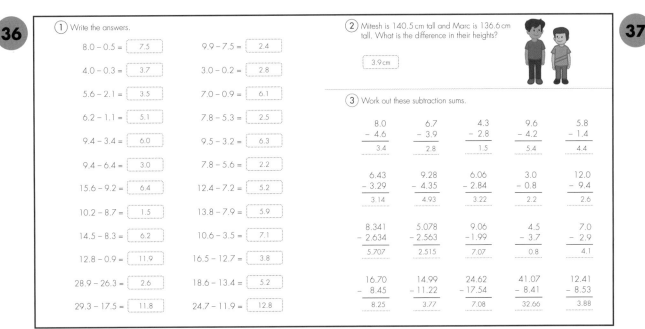

74

Answers:

38–39 Subtraction 2
40–41 Beat the clock 2, see p.80
42–43 Multiplication 1

38

① Write the answers.

5.347	8.231	7.453	2.951	6.523
− 3.200	− 7.003	− 4.560	− 1.460	− 0.692
2.147	1.228	2.893	1.491	5.831

12.949	78.623	52.070	27.511	69.653
− 4.480	− 29.860	− 14.000	− 13.700	− 5.170
8.469	48.763	38.070	13.811	64.483

23.000	85.000	42.000	78.000	35.000
− 7.260	− 43.410	− 18.244	− 42.568	− 17.622
15.740	41.590	23.756	35.432	17.378

34.060	49.768	23.453	55.172	18.643
− 18.040	− 26.769	− 15.564	− 38.081	− 11.931
16.020	22.999	7.889	17.091	6.712

10.000	20.000	30.000	40.000	60.000
− 4.560	− 17.641	− 20.888	− 27.135	− 34.259
5.440	2.359	9.112	12.865	25.741

39

② Answer these questions.

Decrease 4.7 cm by 3.8 cm. [0.9 cm]

What is £12 minus £3.48? [£8.52]

③ Decrease each length by 0.36 m.

5 m [4.64 m]   4.8 m [4.44 m]   3.1 m [2.74 m]

④ A path was 7.82 m long. 1.45 m of it was grassed over. What is the length of the path now? [6.37 m]

⑤ Billy had £42.70 but he spent £6.50. How much money does Billy have now? [£36.20]

⑥ Middle Brook Street was 5.85 m wide. A new brick wall reduced the width by 0.68 m. How wide is the street now? [5.17 m]

⑦ Sandy takes £10.00 out of the bank and then gives 75 p to charity. How much money is Sandy left with? [£9.25]

Care needs to be taken as your child is introduced to trickier subtraction problems. If a sum is answered wrongly, go through it with your child and make sure he or she understands where the mistake has occurred.

42

① Multiply each number by 10.

5.0 [50]   7.5 [75]   8.6 [86]   0.3 [3]

4.2 [42]   0.8 [8]   7.1 [71]   5.7 [57]

7.44 [74.4]   9.25 [92.5]   3.09 [30.9]   5.12 [51.2]

3.17 [31.7]   0.71 [7.1]   8.54 [85.4]   0.89 [8.9]

2.645 [26.45]   7.321 [73.21]   76.342 [763.42]   41.545 [415.45]

② Multiply each number by 100.

3.4 [340]   6.8 [680]   7.1 [710]   5.2 [520]

6.0 [600]   2.7 [270]   9.9 [990]   1.01 [101]

8.27 [827]   4.86 [486]   12.7 [1270]   13.1 [1310]

5.887 [588.7]   5.854 [585.4]   34.22 [3 422]   75.734 [7 573.4]

43.882 [4 388.2]   33.297 [3 329.7]   423.67 [42 367]   123.78 [12 378]

43

③ Multiply each number by 1 000.

5.6 [5 600]   7.1 [7 100]   9.6 [9 600]   4.0 [4 000]

4.3 [4 300]   9.2 [9 200]   8.1 [8 100]   6.8 [6 800]

8.3 [8 300]   0.001 [1]   0.07 [70]   53.999 [53 999]

25.19 [25 190]   32.132 [32 132]   54.67 [54 670]   729.7 [729 700]

403.2 [403 200]   341.56 [341 560]   432.11 [432 110]   345.678 [345 678]

④ Write the answers.

320.006 x 10 [3 200.06]   32.143 x 100 [3 214.3]

29.15 x 1 000 [29 150]   201.12 x 10 [2 011.2]

17.487 x 1 000 [17 487]   56.195 x 100 [5 619.5]

121.165 x 100 [12 116.5]   782.01 x 1 000 [782 010]

812.84 x 100 [81 284]   297.49 x 1 000 [297 490]

253.786 x 10 [2 537.86]   723.707 x 10 [7 237.07]

Your child may be taught some helpful "tricks" to work out this sort of multiplication. It is important for him or her to understand that when multiplying by 10, each number "grows" or is enlarged by a factor of 10.

Answers:

44–45 Division and rounding 1
46–47 Multiplication 2

44

1 What is the place value of 7 in each of these numbers?

2.07	17.63	24.897	315.74
Hundredth	Unit	Thousandth	Tenth

7.12	12.37	70.139	29.871
Unit	Hundredth	Ten	Hundredth

2 Divide each number by 10.

0.07 [0.007]   80.0 [8]   83.86 [8.386]   132.678 [13.2678]

24.8 [2.48]   63.96 [6.396]   4.331 [0.4331]   87.2 [8.72]

18.4 [1.84]   79.12 [7.912]   5.211 [0.5211]   325.986 [32.5986]

3 Divide each number by 100.

603.4 [6.034]   720.05 [7.2005]   3 300.8 [33.008]   200.005 [2.00005]

65.2 [0.652]   7 324.45 [73.2445]   723.966 [7.23966]   53.06 [0.5306]

6.45 [0.0645]   7.83 [0.0783]   34.32 [0.3432]   8.64 [0.0864]

45

4 Divide each number by 1 000.

6.3 [0.0063]   73.85 [0.07385]   923.357 [0.923357]   1 854.6 [1.8546]

0.4 [0.0004]   18.0 [0.018]   75.94 [0.07594]   50.67 [0.05067]

5 At the zoo, Eliza the Elephant weighs 3 750 kg. Billy the Bear is 0.1 (one-tenth), Chai the Cheetah is 0.01 (one-hundredth) and Polly the Penguin is 0.001 (one-thousandth) of Eliza's weight. How much does each animal weigh?

Chai the Cheetah [37.5 kg]   Polly the Penguin [3.75 kg]   Billy the Bear [375 kg]

6 Round each of these numbers to the nearest whole number.

66.67 [67]   3.52 [4]   253.91 [254]   504.54 [505]

25.35 [25]   4.15 [4]   621.32 [621]   698.35 [698]

48.01 [48]   3.89 [4]   481.69 [482]   523.78 [524]

A clear understanding of what dividing by 10, 100 and 1 000 actually means will help a great deal. Your child will need to be very careful with some of these. These pages also include extra practice in place values and rounding to the nearest whole number.

46

1 Write the answers.

4.2 x 6 = [25.2]   2.6 x 8 = [20.8]   3.1 x 2 = [6.2]

5.9 x 6 = [35.4]   9.6 x 8 = [76.8]   1.8 x 9 = [16.2]

3.8 x 7 = [26.6]   6.6 x 4 = [26.4]   2.9 x 8 = [23.2]

4.7 x 9 = [42.3]   5.98 x 5 = [29.9]   7.13 x 6 = [42.78]

8.15 x 7 = [57.05]   3.65 x 4 = [14.6]   9.64 x 2 = [19.28]

4.56 x 3 = [13.68]   8.24 x 2 = [16.48]   9.66 x 4 = [38.64]

5.69 x 3 = [17.07]   8.64 x 7 = [60.48]   7.04 x 5 = [35.2]

3.08 x 9 = [27.72]   7.68 x 6 = [46.08]   8.98 x 9 = [80.82]

0.65 x 5 = [3.25]   1.06 x 7 = [7.42]   6.74 x 7 = [47.18]

9.81 x 7 = [68.67]   8.07 x 8 = [64.56]   9.36 x 4 = [37.44]

8.05 x 3 = [24.15]   1.09 x 6 = [6.54]   9.99 x 5 = [49.95]

47

2 Work out these multiplication sums.

6.23 x 12 = 74.76	7.98 x 18 = 143.64	8.56 x 24 = 205.44	2.66 x 31 = 82.46
4.07 x 52 = 211.64	3.82 x 68 = 259.76	9.27 x 42 = 389.34	6.07 x 64 = 388.48
9.99 x 85 = 849.15	5.08 x 59 = 299.72	1.92 x 13 = 24.96	4.15 x 16 = 66.4
7.19 x 19 = 136.61	1.39 x 14 = 19.46	2.81 x 37 = 103.97	7.75 x 45 = 348.75

3 Simone gets £3.55 as pocket money every week, whereas Charlie gets £16.50 each month. Who gets the most in a year?

Charlie

As with so much of mathematics, instant and quick recall of times tables is essential. It can be very helpful if your child works out an estimated answer before starting a sum. It need not take more than a couple of seconds and can really help if the answer is a long way off.

Answers:

48–49 Division
50–51 Division and rounding 2

48

① Write the answers.

$6.4 ÷ 8 =$ 0.8 $9.6 ÷ 8 =$ 1.2 $7.2 ÷ 9 =$ 0.8

$0.4 ÷ 4 =$ 0.1 $1.7 ÷ 10 =$ 0.17 $0.3 ÷ 10 =$ 0.03

$4.9 ÷ 7 =$ 0.7 $0.36 ÷ 2 =$ 0.18 $0.72 ÷ 12 =$ 0.06

$4.2 ÷ 10 =$ 0.42 $0.48 ÷ 6 =$ 0.08 $0.36 ÷ 4 =$ 0.09

$0.75 ÷ 5 =$ 0.15 $1.08 ÷ 9 =$ 0.12 $1.21 ÷ 11 =$ 0.11

$0.54 ÷ 6 =$ 0.09 $7.28 ÷ 8 =$ 0.91 $8.19 ÷ 9 =$ 0.91

$4.97 ÷ 7 =$ 0.71 $2.46 ÷ 6 =$ 0.41 $4.84 ÷ 4 =$ 1.21

② Emily, Tom and Sky have a jumble sale and make £152.25. The money is divided equally between five charities. How much does each charity receive?

£30.45

49

③ Write the answers.

$4.32 ÷ 9 =$ 0.48 $13.8 ÷ 6 =$ 2.3 $27.3 ÷ 7 =$ 3.9

$16.3 ÷ 5 =$ 3.26 $32.8 ÷ 4 =$ 8.2 $77.4 ÷ 9 =$ 8.6

$64.6 ÷ 8 =$ 8.075 $48.1 ÷ 5 =$ 9.62 $81.9 ÷ 9 =$ 9.1

$87.5 ÷ 7 =$ 12.5 $29.7 ÷ 4 =$ 7.425 $46.8 ÷ 4 =$ 11.7

$89.7 ÷ 3 =$ 29.9 $93.5 ÷ 2 =$ 46.75 $69.3 ÷ 3 =$ 23.1

$88.4 ÷ 4 =$ 22.1 $12.99 ÷ 6 =$ 2.165 $16.56 ÷ 8 =$ 2.07

$28.15 ÷ 5 =$ 5.63 $22.76 ÷ 4 =$ 5.69 $39.12 ÷ 3 =$ 13.04

$53.92 ÷ 8 =$ 6.74 $63.27 ÷ 9 =$ 7.03 $61.12 ÷ 8 =$ 7.64

$53.12 ÷ 8 =$ 6.64 $76.44 ÷ 6 =$ 12.74 $72.36 ÷ 4 =$ 18.09

$75.45 ÷ 5 =$ 15.09 $72.24 ÷ 6 =$ 12.04 $60.41 ÷ 10 =$ 6.041

$80.15 ÷ 7 =$ 11.45 $102.2 ÷ 7 =$ 14.6 $104.8 ÷ 2 =$ 52.4

Times tables knowledge is essential once again. Have your child make a quick estimate of the answer by rounding the figure. For example, $\frac{1.9}{8}$ can be thought of as $\frac{2}{10}$, giving an estimate of 0.2 with the exact answer 0.23.

50

① Work out each division and round the answer to the nearest penny.

£7 ÷ 3	£15 ÷ 7	£31 ÷ 5	£47 ÷ 3
233p	214p	620p	1 567p

£18.50 ÷ 3	£2.43 ÷ 6	£7.42 ÷ 9	£7.32 ÷ 4
617p	41p	82p	183p

£0.75 ÷ 4	£1.50 ÷ 7	£3 ÷ 9	£2.99 ÷ 4
19p	21p	33p	75p

② Work out each division and round the answer to the nearest centimetre.
(Hint: 100 cm = 1 m)

9 m ÷ 7	16 m ÷ 6	45 m ÷ 4	69 m ÷ 2
129 cm	267 cm	1 125 cm	3 450 cm

7 m ÷ 3	26 m ÷ 4	69 m ÷ 5	72 m ÷ 7
233 cm	650 cm	1 380 cm	1 029 cm

3.6 m ÷ 5	4.28 m ÷ 3	12.65 m ÷ 6	7.4 m ÷ 3
72 cm	143 cm	211 cm	247 cm

12.9 m ÷ 8	8.12 m ÷ 5	18.8 m ÷ 6	25.6 m ÷ 7
161 cm	162 cm	313 cm	366 cm

51

③ Work out each division and round the answer to the nearest gram.
(Hint: 1 000 g = 1 kg)

4 kg ÷ 6	19 kg ÷ 9	23 kg ÷ 12	12 kg ÷ 7
667 g	2 111 g	1 917 g	1 714 g

4.7 kg ÷ 6	11.9 kg ÷ 9	18.4 kg ÷ 7	16.9 kg ÷ 3
783 g	1 322 g	2 629 g	5 633 g

④ Work out each division and round the answer to the nearest metre.
(Hint: 1 000 m = 1 km)

2 km ÷ 3	17 km ÷ 8	38 km ÷ 6	33 km ÷ 5
667 m	2 125 m	6 333 m	6 600 m

1.78 km ÷ 4	2.06 km ÷ 9	3.63 km ÷ 5	20.4 km ÷ 7
445 m	229 m	726 m	2 914 m

⑤ Work out each division and round the answer to the nearest millilitre.
(Hint: 1 000 ml = 1 l)

8 l ÷ 6	13 l ÷ 4	40 l ÷ 7	46 l ÷ 8
1 333 ml	3 250 ml	5 714 ml	5 750 ml

23 l ÷ 9	43 l ÷ 5	62 l ÷ 3	17 l ÷ 8
2 556 ml	8 600 ml	20 667 ml	2 125 ml

Care needs to be taken with the units in these questions. For example, a question may be set in kilometres but the answer will be required in metres. A calculator may be used for some of the questions, but make sure your child is able to work out the answers without a calculator.

Answers:

52–53 Division and rounding 3
54–55 Decimals and percentages 1

52

① Work out each answer and round to the nearest pound.

£17.89 ÷ 3	£26.50 ÷ 4	£30 ÷ 7	£37.15 ÷ 6
£6	£7	£4	£6

£275 ÷ 3	£723 ÷ 6	£26 ÷ 6	£295 ÷ 4
£92	£121	£4	£74

② Work out each answer and round to the nearest metre.

34.8 m ÷ 7	41.9 m ÷ 7	60.34 m ÷ 4	28.4 m ÷ 3
5 m	6 m	15 m	9 m

2 364 m ÷ 7	406 m ÷ 14	3 186 m ÷ 12	5 123 m ÷ 11
338 m	29 m	266 m	466 m

③ Work out each answer and round to the nearest centimetre.

253 cm ÷ 7	4.12 m ÷ 7	372 cm ÷ 5	789 cm ÷ 7
36 cm	59 cm	74 cm	113 cm

89 cm ÷ 3	1.42 m ÷ 7	56.86 cm ÷ 4	14.19 cm ÷ 5
30 cm	20 cm	14 cm	3 cm

53

④ Work out each division and round to the nearest gram.

43 g ÷ 2	317 g ÷ 6	500 g ÷ 6
22 g	53 g	83 g

534 g ÷ 7	2.5 kg ÷ 9	890 g ÷ 12
76 g	278 g	74 g

⑤ Work out each division and round to the nearest penny. Answer in pounds.

£2 ÷ 3	£53.60 ÷ 7	£120 ÷ 11	£28.30 ÷ 9
£0.67	£7.66	£10.91	£3.14

£85.62 ÷ 4	£49.12 ÷ 6	£59.52 ÷ 3	£72.12 ÷ 8
£21.41	£8.19	£19.84	£9.02

⑥ Work out each division and round to the nearest litre.

582 l ÷ 5	20.1 l ÷ 3	324 l ÷ 6	429 l ÷ 7
116 l	7 l	54 l	61 l

456 l ÷ 5	63.85 l ÷ 3	10.02 l ÷ 6	256 l ÷ 7
91 l	21 l	2 l	37 l

These calculations can take a long time, more than ten minutes. Have your child show a few non-calculator workings and then do the rest with a calculator. Be very careful with the units being used.

54

① What is 70% of each amount?

£6	£23	6.5 m	37 m
£4.20	£16.10	4.55 m	25.9 m

② Write each decimal as its percentage equivalent.

0.75	0.45	0.333	0.125
75%	45%	33.3%	12.5%

0.01	0.9	0.375	0.3
1%	90%	37.5%	30%

③ Write each percentage in its decimal form.

55%	25%	12.5%	5%
0.55	0.25	0.125	0.05

65%	40%	80%	95%
0.65	0.4	0.8	0.95

④ What is 35% of each amount?

6 m	4 km	£12	7 m
2.1 m	1.4 km	£4.20	2.45 m

55

⑤ What is 5% of each amount?

£16	200 m	£4.60	60 m
£0.80	10 m	£0.23	3 m

⑥ What percentage of 200 is each of the following?

50	10	75	150
25%	5%	37.5%	75%

⑦ What percentage of 5 m is each of the following?

50 cm	20 cm	25 cm	2 m
10%	4%	5%	40%

⑧ What percentage of £5 is each of the following?

£1	£3	£4.50	10 p
20%	60%	90%	2%

⑨ What percentage of 150 is each of the following?

30	15	45	90
20%	10%	30%	60%

By this time, your child should have a very good knowledge and understanding of percentages and decimals and the relationship between them. This should help him or her develop quick and accurate methods for solving problems such as working out 50 cm as a percentage of 5 m.

Answers:

56–57 Decimals and percentages 2
58–59 Estimation and rounding

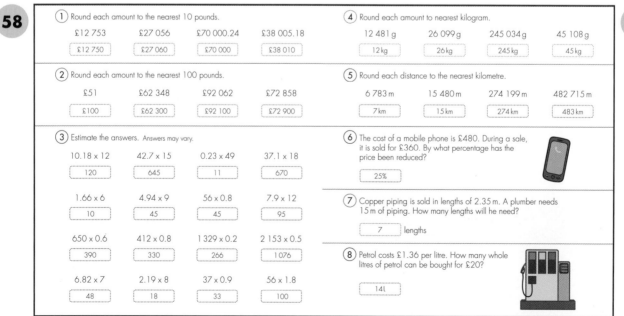

56

1. A motorway was originally 40 km long but has had its length increased to 60 km. By what percentage has the motorway increased in length?

   50%

2. David usually receives £5 pocket money per week, but on his tenth birthday he had the amount raised by 10%. How much pocket money will David receive now?

   £5.50

3. Sean measured himself on his ninth birthday and was 120 cm tall. On his tenth birthday, he measured himself again and this time he was 144 cm tall. By what percentage has Sean grown?

   20%

4. A container carries 2 000 new television sets. When it was opened, 0.05 of the televisions were broken. How many television sets have not been broken?

   1 900   television sets

5. Emmie usually spends £80 a week on food shopping. Before Christmas, she increased this amount by 0.25. How much money will Emmie spend now?

   £100

57

6. Victoria sends 500 texts per month. While on holiday this number decreases by 70%. How many texts does Victoria send while on holiday?

   150   texts

7. A television programme lasts for one hour, but 0.125 of this time is taken up by advertisements. How long is the programme without the advertisements?

   52.5 minutes

8. What percentage of £1 000 is £50?

   5%

9. The area of a football pitch in a stadium is 8 000 m². After alterations, the area is reduced by 15%. What is the new area of the pitch?

   6 800 m²

10. An amount of money is increased by 35% and is now £27. How much was the amount before the increase?

    £20

These questions are put into realistic situations and require your child to work out the operations needed to solve each one. The child must read the question very carefully to see exactly what is being asked for.

58

1. Round each amount to the nearest 10 pounds.

£12 753	£27 056	£70 000.24	£38 005.18
£12 750	£27 060	£70 000	£38 010

2. Round each amount to the nearest 100 pounds.

£51	£62 348	£92 062	£72 858
£100	£62 300	£92 100	£72 900

3. Estimate the answers. Answers may vary.

10.18 × 12	42.7 × 15	0.23 × 49	37.1 × 18
120	645	11	670

1.66 × 6	4.94 × 9	56 × 0.8	7.9 × 12
10	45	45	95

650 × 0.6	412 × 0.8	1 329 × 0.2	2 153 × 0.5
390	330	266	1 076

6.82 × 7	2.19 × 8	37 × 0.9	56 × 1.8
48	18	33	100

59

4. Round each amount to nearest kilogram.

12 481 g	26 099 g	245 034 g	45 108 g
12 kg	26 kg	245 kg	45 kg

5. Round each distance to the nearest kilometre.

6 783 m	15 480 m	274 199 m	482 715 m
7 km	15 km	274 km	483 km

6. The cost of a mobile phone is £480. During a sale, it is sold for £360. By what percentage has the price been reduced?

   25%

7. Copper piping is sold in lengths of 2.35 m. A plumber needs 15 m of piping. How many lengths will he need?

   7   lengths

8. Petrol costs £1.36 per litre. How many whole litres of petrol can be bought for £20?

   14 L

Your child can work out his or her own estimation methods. Depending on the method he or she chooses, the answers may vary. So, the answers here are only generalisations of what should be expected.

Answers:

60–61 Solving problems 1
62–63 Solving problems 2
64–65 Beat the clock 3, see p.80

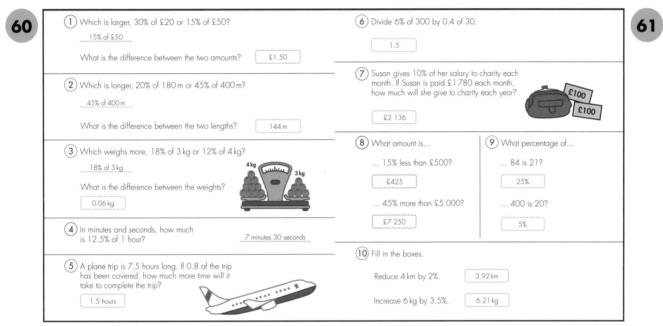

60

1. Which is larger, 30% of £20 or 15% of £50?

   15% of £50

   What is the difference between the two amounts? £1.50

2. Which is longer, 20% of 180 m or 45% of 400 m?

   45% of 400 m

   What is the difference between the two lengths? 144 m

3. Which weighs more, 18% of 3 kg or 12% of 4 kg?

   18% of 3 kg

   What is the difference between the weights? 0.06 kg

4. In minutes and seconds, how much is 12.5% of 1 hour? 7 minutes 30 seconds

5. A plane trip is 7.5 hours long. If 0.8 of the trip has been covered, how much more time will it take to complete the trip? 1.5 hours

61

6. Divide 6% of 300 by 0.4 of 30. 1.5

7. Susan gives 10% of her salary to charity each month. If Susan is paid £1780 each month, how much will she give to charity each year? £2 136

8. What amount is…
   … 15% less than £500? £425
   … 45% more than £5 000? £7 250

9. What percentage of…
   … 84 is 21? 25%
   … 400 is 20? 5%

10. Fill in the boxes.
    Reduce 4 km by 2%. 3.92 km
    Increase 6 kg by 3.5%. 6.21 kg

Your child is provided with word problems to understand decimal calculations in real life. He or she must read the question very carefully to ensure he or she is giving the answer correctly.

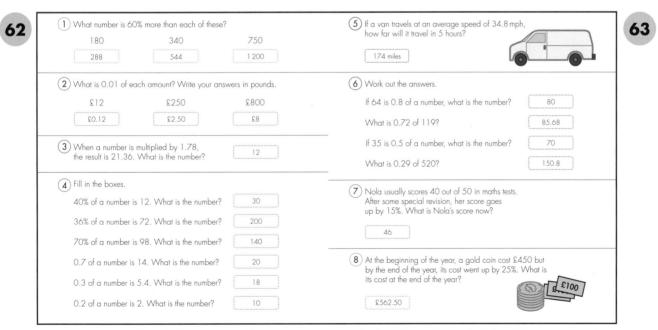

62

1. What number is 60% more than each of these?
180	340	750
288	544	1 200

2. What is 0.01 of each amount? Write your answers in pounds.
£12	£250	£800
£0.12	£2.50	£8

3. When a number is multiplied by 1.78, the result is 21.36. What is the number? 12

4. Fill in the boxes.
   40% of a number is 12. What is the number? 30
   36% of a number is 72. What is the number? 200
   70% of a number is 98. What is the number? 140
   0.7 of a number is 14. What is the number? 20
   0.3 of a number is 5.4. What is the number? 18
   0.2 of a number is 2. What is the number? 10

63

5. If a van travels at an average speed of 34.8 mph, how far will it travel in 5 hours? 174 miles

6. Work out the answers.
   If 64 is 0.8 of a number, what is the number? 80
   What is 0.72 of 119? 85.68
   If 35 is 0.5 of a number, what is the number? 70
   What is 0.29 of 520? 150.8

7. Nola usually scores 40 out of 50 in maths tests. After some special revision, her score goes up by 15%. What is Nola's score now? 46

8. At the beginning of the year, a gold coin cost £450 but by the end of the year, its cost went up by 25%. What is its cost at the end of the year? £562.50

These questions mainly include operations like multiplication and division. Some of these calculations are fairly tricky and your child should be encouraged to think them through carefully.

Answers:

20–21 Beat the clock 1
40–41 Beat the clock 2
64–65 Beat the clock 3

These "Beat the clock" pages test your child's ability to quickly recall the lessons learned. The tests require your child to work under some pressure. As with most tests of this type, tell your child before he or she starts not to get stuck on one question, but to move on and return to the tricky one later if time allows. Encourage your child to record his or her score and the time taken to complete the test, then to retake the test later to see if he or she can improve on his or her previous attempt.

20 / 21

(1) 0.25	(2) 0.75	(3) 0.5
(4) 0.4	(5) 0.8	(6) 0.2
(7) 0.6	(8) 0.9	(9) 0.1
(10) 0.7	(11) 0.4	(12) 0.5
(13) 0.6	(14) 0.8	(15) 0.3
(16) 0.7	(17) 1.8	(18) 1.2
(19) 2.1	(20) 0.2	(21) 0.5
(22) 1.1	(23) 3.0	(24) 5.0
(25) 0.6	(26) 40.0	(27) 15.0
(28) 36.0	(29) 70.0	(30) 49.0
(31) 5.67	(32) 4.97	(33) 1.64
(34) 8.52	(35) 12.97	(36) 1.35
(37) 8.05	(38) 9.43	(39) 0.66
(40) 7	(41) 8	(42) 3
(43) 8	(44) 8	(45) 10
(46) 22	(47) 37	(48) 4
(49) $\frac{75}{100}$	(50) $\frac{96}{100}$	(51) $\frac{2}{100}$
(52) $\frac{25}{100}$	(53) $\frac{675}{1\,000}$	(54) $\frac{8}{1\,000}$
(55) $\frac{30}{100}$	(56) $\frac{3}{1\,000}$	(57) $\frac{5}{10}$

40 / 41

(1) 9.1	(2) 5.9	(3) 10.6
(4) 12.9	(5) 10	(6) 9
(7) 9	(8) 8	(9) 11.2
(10) 14.1	(11) 7.5	(12) 6.6
(13) 6.5	(14) 10.9	(15) 6.1
(16) 1.7	(17) 5.1	(18) 12.7
(19) 7.4	(20) 10.46	(21) 1
(22) 3.1	(23) 7.77	(24) 10.61
(25) 12.94	(26) 8.42	(27) 9.21
(28) 11.72		
(29) 4.8	(30) 5.7	(31) 1.2
(32) 9	(33) 3.2	(34) 6.8
(35) 7.1	(36) 1.1	(37) 6
(38) 13.7	(39) 1.1	(40) 2.2
(41) £1.25	(42) £12	(43) £4.75
(44) £0.80	(45) 1.8 m	(46) £0.21
(47) 0.12 m	(48) £0.32	(49) £1.95
(50) 0.5	(51) 0.1	(52) 0.7
(53) 0.15	(54) 0.05	(55) 0.45
(56) 0.9	(57) 0.34	(58) 0.01

64 / 65

(1) 75.0	(2) 168.0	(3) 0.3
(4) 709	(5) 2 405	(6) 306
(7) 500	(8) 3 880	(9) 100 100
(10) 0.46	(11) 6.01	(12) 10.3
(13) 0.16	(14) 42.5	(15) 0.3005
(16) 43.967	(17) 132.9	(18) 78.519
(19) 4.89	(20) 6.89	(21) 8.01
(22) 17.01	(23) 31.42	(24) 24.44
(25) 65.01	(26) 80.01	(27) 236.99
(28) 2.875	(29) 0.556	(30) 1.001
(31) 52.050	(32) 6.351	(33) 28.689
(34) 1.2	(35) 14.4	(36) 4.8
(37) 13.5	(38) 15	(39) 300
(40) 15.2	(41) 1.4	(42) 0.09
(43) 6	(44) 0.28	(45) 18
(46) 0.25	(47) 180	(48) 225